George Parsons Lathrop

Newport

George Parsons Lathrop

Newport

ISBN/EAN: 9783337156527

Printed in Europe, USA, Canada, Australia, Japan

Cover: Foto ©Andreas Hilbeck / pixelio.de

More available books at **www.hansebooks.com**

BY

GEORGE PARSONS LATHROP

NEW YORK
CHARLES SCRIBNER'S SONS
1884

COPYRIGHT, 1884, BY
CHARLES SCRIBNER'S SONS.

𝔉ranklin 𝔓ress:
RAND, AVERY, AND COMPANY,
BOSTON.

CONTENTS.

		PAGE
I.	"Forty — Love"	3
II.	The Life of a Letter	23
III.	Mrs. Blazer's Dinner	44
IV.	Some Important Trifles	64
V.	A Woman's Agony	78
VI.	Dewdrops and Diamonds	95
VII.	Lord Hawkstane's Just Pride	119
VIII.	Half-Lights	131
IX.	Polo, and Certain Possibilities	147
X.	Young Thorburn and Old Thorburn	162
XI.	Oliphant, Octavia, and Josephine	180
XII.	In the Footsteps of Fate	196
XIII.	Hawks and Doves	208
XIV.	The Flight of a Meteor	217
XV.	A Man's Ordeal	233
XVI.	Little Effie	250
XVII.	Repentance	261
XVIII.	The Night-Voyage	271
XIX.	Love at Last	285

NEWPORT.

I.

"FORTY — LOVE."

AT the beginning of the Newport season there is a gentle novelty about the surroundings, even to those who are most familiar with them: indeed, for the moment, it closely resembles the surprise of a discovery.

"Don't you think so?" Mrs. Deering asked her cousin Oliphant. They were walking together through the Casino grounds, and had just taken some chairs on the inner lawn. "I've always found it so. How is it, Eugene, with you?"

Her vivacious, rosy face, as she put the question, made more impression on him than her remark.

"I have no experience," he said; "it is so long, you know, since I was here last, and every thing was different then." Perhaps it occurred to Mrs. Deering that, under the term "every thing," he included many circumstances of deeper moment than mere outward changes; but she went on as if these had no place in his thoughts: "This establishment is so recent that it can't be a very old story even to you. I certainly feel the novelty you speak of; but will it go on? That's what I want to know. If it will, I shall be grateful to Newport."

"Ah, now you are asking too much," said his cousin, bestowing upon him so much of reproof as the sparkling contentment in her young eyes would consent to. "I hope you're not going to begin sighing, after my advising you to come here. Please observe that it isn't flattering to me."

"True," said Oliphant, smiling; "you might construe it so. Well, you sha'n't hear a murmur. Not a drum shall be heard, nor a funeral note escape me."

"I should trust they wouldn't," Mrs. Deering exclaimed. "You really have no cause to complain, Eugene. You are well off; you are still young;" and she was considering whether to add "you are handsome," when he cut short the enumeration.

"Not so very youthful," he said. "There is a great difference between being 'still young,' and young without any adverb. When you put that in, you clap on about ten years at one stroke."

"Well," replied Mrs. Deering, taking advantage of the chance, "even ten years can't make it so very bad. How old are you, really?"

Oliphant affected to ponder. "That," he said, "is one of the great mysteries of the period. I may be able to tell you, though, some day or other."

She knew, however, that he had probably entered his fortieth year; and in fact there were little glintings of silver white here and there in the comely chestnut hue of the thick, short, curling hair beneath his hat-brim. The tolerant sun disclosing these was not more indifferent to their presence than Oliphant: as for Mary Deering, she thought they added distinction to his fine bearing and strong, quiet face. So did other people. It may be said here that, although Oliphant had been for three years a widower, women of undoubted attractiveness had several times, without his being aware of it, made him the object of sentimental reveries. At this very moment, his cousin, who from her point of view as a married woman was quite disinterested, busied herself with a silent inquiry as to whether he had positively decided never to wed again; being convinced that if he persisted in such a decision it would be a great pity.

From where they sat they caught, through the curious lattice-work of the dark Horseshoe Gallery, a glimpse of the clock-tower, with its gilded dial, above the verdant, fountained quadrangle; on the other side they had in near view the brown galleries and brick front of the theatre and racket-court, near which, in an additional enclosure, were a number of lawn-tennis players; limber young men and picturesque, — some in white flannel, others with long scarlet stockings, colored belts or dark sashes, and white hats bent down towards their ears, like the petasus of Mercury shorn of its wings. The two listened to the low twang of the rackets in the hands of these players, alternating with strains of the lightest possible music from one corner of the balcony; waltzes and French opera, inspired by a witticism and beaten up, if that were conceivable, with white of egg. A brilliant sunlight streamed over every thing, touching the shingle roofs with bright grays, making vivid the summer trees that stood golden-green side by side with heavy conifers; and from that portion of the building devoted to the Casino Club a dormer appeared to be winking, with a combination of mediæval and of Yankee humor. There was a mixture in the architecture; at all events, a hint of something old English, something Nüremberg-like, and something Japanese.

"This is a fascinating piece of work," Oliphant remarked, looking around; "a delightful mimicry of I don't exactly know what. There's an affectation, perhaps, in staining the wood to make it look old, but the whole thing seems to be unique; and it's like Newport. For Newport has its own atmosphere, and yet you feel that it is always imitating something else."

"I'm not sure you do justice either to the building or to Newport," answered his cousin, dissentingly. "They're both delightful; so what is the use of trying to pick some flaw? That's the way we're always spoiling our enjoyment of things, nowadays; or, if we don't, some critic does it for us under the pretence that he was born for the purpose. Are *you* going to assume that *rôle?*"

"Fate has played the critic with me, and taught me how," was Oliphant's reply. "When circumstances have always forced me to see the flaws in life, how can you expect that I shouldn't form the habit of looking for them a little in every thing?"

"Oh, you are a dreadful, horrible cynic," said his cousin, concentrating the quick, soft lines of her small face upon him, in an amusing glance mingled of horror and beaming approval. "This is just the way you talk about every thing."

Eugene merely laughed. "Shall I keep silent, then?" he asked.

"Yes," said Mrs. Deering, with despotic promptness.

They remained a while without speaking. As water flowing against a rock wears wave-lines into it, so a person who has been much alone has the marks of solitude worn into his being. Traces of that slow erosion were discernible in Oliphant's face when in repose, showing with what force silent experiences had wrought upon it. His light-hearted cousin was not much inclined to analyze what she saw there; probably she could not have done so if she had tried; but as she scrutinized him sidewise at this moment, something made her think of his past. She remembered how he had gone very early into a business life, and had had to toil desperately until within a short time; but that was nothing: had not Roger, her husband, done the same? and he was still toiling, while Eugene, after becoming a bankrupt, had recovered, and by a lucky hit leaped into independence. She remembered, further, how she had always supposed him to be unhappy with his wife; he had been mis-mated. But there, again, how fortunate! Was he not free, with many advantages should he wish to make a happier match, and well provided for living by himself if he preferred what she thought so regrettable a state? Life is so simple — when we don't have to live it ourselves.

Grievances are noisy: griefs are little heard from. Luckily we cannot trundle our sorrows about in plain sight, when we go walking; hence Mary Deering was not made uncomfortable by knowing just what was in Oliphant's mind; and the people who kept assembling more and more in the Casino, while these two sat there, were able to display themselves one to another with an unconcern as suave as if they had borrowed their minds, no less than their trim attire, from the latest fashion-plates. Pretty sight it was: how placid they looked! Eugene fondly believed them all much happier than himself; he was young enough for that, you see. But Mrs. Deering was the first to resume conversation, which she did by commenting on an individual here and there.

Eugene, having grown absent-minded, only half heard her. He was humming under his breath an old ballad, the words of which that came to him, though he did not utter them, ran thus: —

> "An' I were as fair as she,
> Or she were as kind as I;
> What pair could have made, as we,
> So pretty a sympathie!"

What glimmer of recollection, what sunken hope, brought this tune into his mind? He was roused by his cousin's sharper accent.

"Look, Eugene! I want you to notice these people."

"Which? Coming along the path here?"

"Yes; the lady in front is Mrs. Farley Blazer." He beheld a large, stout woman with a smoky white face and quietly but not well dressed, who moved with slow grandeur, as if in her youth she had been swan-like, and had not quite forgotten the fact. "And the gentleman is old Dana Sweetser. Doesn't look old, does he? Those two younger women, behind, are her nieces." The two girls referred to, though not beyond question pretty, evidently made great claim to style; and, swimming in the wake of their majestic aunt, were trying in their limited way to be swan-like also.

Mrs. Deering exchanged a smile and a bow with the group; but as they passed away again, she said to Oliphant, "That woman is what I call a social usurper. She came here years ago and tried to impose herself on the world by a *coup d'état*. There was a bitter resistance, but slowly and surely she has borne it down, and seems to be settled on her throne."

"And Sweetser?" asked Oliphant, mildly amused. "What about him?"

"Oh, he's good style; good family, and all that; but principally he's a sentimental old beau. He divides his time between organizing societies for Promoting the Importance of Members, and falling in love. He will pass through half a dozen rhapsodical affairs, this summer. Poor Dana!"

She had barely finished speaking when they observed a slender young man, with a single eye-glass and a long coat, who stiffly carried a thin stick, approaching them from the racket-court. Just as he came opposite them, a white ball bounding from the tennis-ground flew towards him, at an angle threatening mischief to his tall hat. He dodged it, and it struck the sward near enough to bounce again in the direction of Mary Deering. The slender young man darted vainly forward, to arrest this perplexing missile before it should reach her; but though he bent down with commendable promptness, it escaped him and grazed her chair. At the same instant he found himself landing on one knee, to avoid a fall, and gazing anxiously towards her. He took off his hat.

"Attitude of devotion!" he exclaimed in a subdued voice, with what was meant to pass for well-regulated humor. Even in these few words, however, he contrived to let his perfected English accent manifest itself. "Good morning, Mrs. Deering," he added, more formally, straightening himself up again.

"Good morning, Mr. Atlee." She made the two men acquainted, briefly. "You couldn't have done that better if you'd been on the stage," she said.

"It hardly counts in the game, I suppose," said Oliphant, picking up the grass-stained ball, which he threw to the players.

Atlee looked at him through his glass, as if he hardly knew how this remark was designed; then he turned the polished disc inquiringly on Mrs. Deering, who smiled with mysterious satisfaction. "Well, no," he said haltingly. "I suppose, Mrs. Deering," he recommenced, "you are coming to the Casino dance, to-night. *On se donne le mot*, you know. Monday is to be *the* night, regularly."

"That will be bad for the ladies who ride, when the

meets begin," said she. "But, of course, I shall come to-night."

Oliphant had given up dancing, and looked upon the artificial fox-hunt with contempt; so he began to feel out of place, and to wish that Atlee would go away. But as the young man did not vanish, our friend adopted the simple expedient of considering him an inferior individual, and withdrew from the conversation, fixing his attention entirely on the tennis. He became oblivious to every thing but the cries of the players: "Net!" — "Fault." — "Thirty, love." — "Deuce." At length these annoyed him, too. "Do you understand the game, Mr. Atlee?" he asked.

"Oh, a trifle," said the young man. "Must do what all the other fools do, you know."

"Naturally," returned Oliphant, with zest.

"Is that the reason you asked him?" Mrs. Deering inquired of her cousin, darting mischief at Atlee. "How clever, when you haven't known him!"

"That's hard," feebly protested her admirer. "Well, you see," he continued, addressing Oliphant with the comprehensiveness of an amateur lecturer, "there are four courts, and one man serves, and" —

"Oh, I don't want a regular exposition," Oliphant interrupted, having reached an advanced stage of unreason. "But it would be a relief if you would tell me what their sentimental phrase 'love' means."

"That's very easy," Atlee said. "It's only a gentle way of saying that one side hasn't won any thing whatever."

"Then, according to this computation, love is nothing."

"Exactly."

"How appropriate! I think better of the game: there must be some sense in it."

"Eugene!" cried Mrs. Deering, in reproof. "I thought I had got you nicely chained up. What do you mean by breaking loose again, and barking like that? Mr. Atlee, my cousin is a cynic."

Thus admonished, Atlee examined him cautiously with his defensive eye-glass.

"None of the other people are sitting down," said Oliphant. "Don't you think we'd better be getting away from here?"

"Forty — love. Game," muttered Atlee, who had again diverted his superb attention to the nearest pair of batters. "That's total defeat, you know," he volunteered for Oliphant's benefit.

Eugene could not help applying this phraseology of the game to his own case. His cousin had, that morning, expatiated to him on the happiness of some friends of hers who had married in middle life; and within a few moments she had questioned him as to his own age. But love and forty made a bad combination in tennis, as they might also in a human career; a combination involving absolute failure on one side.

"We may as well go up on to the balcony, if you want to move," Mrs. Deering said, obligingly; and they all three started in that direction.

The latticed promenade, when they reached it, was crowded, and echoed to a light buzz of rapid talk, salutation, and correct laughter, as if it had been a drawing-room. They paced up and down its length for a few minutes; Oliphant noticing that the space nearer the music was tacitly left to those who were not of the governing social league; persons of unfashionable appearance, many of them passing visitors, who gazed over at the others from a chilly border-land of solitude, as it were, and appeared to be taking the spectacle with a good deal of seriousness, an air of mute and mournful inquiry. Atlee slipped away to speak to a young lady at one side of the gallery: "Vivian Ware," Mrs. Deering specified to her companion. "A charming girl, from Boston. I want you to know her, too."

Beyond doubt, Miss Ware was a most engaging creature, even on a casual glance. She stood by one of the turned posts that upheld the gallery-ceiling, leaning slightly against it and surrounded by several young men,—"That is the Count Fitz-Stuart nearest to her," Oliphant heard his feminine mentor saying,—so that she might have been figured as at bay, making a final stand against her pursuers. But the situation evidently did not disturb her. Slight without suggesting fragility, she showed decided calm and self-possession, but was radiant with expression, and was talking first to one and then to another. Oliphant not being devoid of imagination, it occurred to him that, in her pure white dress wrought with a perfection of skill that made it resemble a natural growth, she might well be compared to a fresh honeysuckle blossom.

"I should like to know her," he said; "but not now. For a while I will just look."

"There'll be plenty of time," his pretty cousin

agreed. " You're like a man who has been starving, and I must be careful with you; too much at once might be your death."

The next instant she was accosted by Mr. Dana Sweetser, who, of a shapely figure, had a light but aged mustache that lay like a withered leaf above his lips and brushed his cheeks, the pink of which was forcing itself out of season. He wore a salmon-tinted sirocco neck-scarf, and apparently was brimming over with compliments.

" A most lovely morning, Mrs. Deering," he exclaimed, poising himself artfully on his thin legs, that terminated in narrow shoes adorned with buff gaiters. " And I assure you one sees it better when it is reflected in a lovely face."

" That's a new sort of barometer," said she, " but not hard to find, here;" and she glanced around.

" Happy to make your acquaintance," Sweetser proceeded as elastically as before, on being presented to Oliphant. " And you have lately arrived? Ah, Newport is the gem of all our watering-places. You will find yourself unable to leave it, Mr. Oliphant. Are you not already charmed?"

" I'm trying to be," replied Oliphant; " and I dare say, if I'm not it won't be the fault of the place."

" You have only to look about you, sir. The most delightful society — people of leisure and cultivation, assembled from the different cities that separate them in winter: Newport claims them all, you see, by natural right. I was about to tell you something, Mrs. Deering," he pursued, turning to her; and Oliphant seized the occasion to move apart.

He had not gone many steps, before he was arrested by the sight of a face that he fancied was familiar to him. It offered a surface epitome of character not distinguished for refinement, but rather forcible than coarse, in spite of a rough-grained complexion and the aggressive bushiness of brown whiskers and a biforked beard. The man was dressed in a blue flannel yachting suit, as if he disdained making much concession to the custom of elaborate toilets. Nevertheless, it was clear that he stood well in the estimation of those around him. He bore signs of mental power, and possessed a cool, ample eye that took in every thing with undisturbed comprehensiveness. We might say it was a peculiarly noiseless eye. Indeed, Oliphant was persuaded that it had encompassed him, as it were, and had fully identified him, an instant or two before any light of recognition was allowed to flash out. But when that preliminary was over, the face became energetic with geniality, and the individual to whom it belonged stepped forward with hand outstretched.

"My dear fellow!" said he, in a hearty, melodious voice that carried conviction with it. "How do you do; and where did you drop from?"

"I thought it was you, Porter," Oliphant responded, oddly feeling that his own heartiness, though he knew it to be genuine, was a mere make-believe or shadow beside the other man's; "but it's such a length of time. . . . I was rather hesitating."

"As the Irishman said," Porter at once rejoined, "when they asked him whether, as a punishment for his crime, he would prefer to go to the gallows or

Australia. He told 'em, you know, he would 'rather hesitate.' Well, where have you been? Tell me all about it? What's the news?"

They began to walk the gallery at the least crowded end, with occasional inroads upon the more fashionable one. It was not a place for clapping a man upon the back; and, for all his force, Porter's manner was perfectly in keeping with the genius of the spot. But Oliphant felt that practically he had been clapped upon the back, and rather liked it: he began to be more at home. He noticed, also, as they passed and repassed, that those who had previously been talking with Porter were now examining himself with an access of interest merging into respect, as they saw the friendly terms on which he stood with the wearer of the blue suit. This roused in Oliphant an internal laughter; but it was agreeable to find that, while still unknown, he could thus enjoy an indirect homage. "I have my foot on the stair," he said to himself.

Meanwhile, two gentlemen who sat together in the shadow, not far from the musicians, fixed their attention on the pair as they receded in their walk.

"Quisbrough," said one of these individuals, — grave, elderly, clad throughout in black and wearing the long-skirted broadcloth of a departing generation, — "isn't that man Porter? Horatio Porter, I mean; commonly known as Raish."

The speaker had a pale, smooth-shaven face, seamed with fine wrinkles arranged on a system which implied in equal measure a great store of legal acumen and much experience of dyspepsia.

"Yes; that's Raish," replied Quisbrough. "But I thought you knew him, Judge: thought everybody knew him, and that you knew everybody."

"Well, you've hit it pretty close," the Judge answered, with a grim smile, restrained by habit. "Of course I know *of* him. A case in which he had an interest came before me, in fact. But he didn't appear but once, and I haven't seen him since. I'm not a brilliant financier, and I'm not a yachtsman, and I'm not a half society man, either; so our lines hardly cross. He certainly is going ahead remarkably, is Raish. What do you think of him?" In saying this, he turned his eyes warily towards Quisbrough.

"I've hardly formed an opinion," said the latter, poking one finger meditatively into the side of his thick, black beard. "He's a friend of old Thorburn's, you know."

"I see; I see," murmured the old gentleman. "Friend of young Thorburn's, too?" he asked.

"Yes," said Quisbrough, still prodding his beard. And they began talking of something else.

"Oh yes, I know the old fellow," Porter was saying at the same moment, in answer to a question from Oliphant. "It's Judge Malachi Hixon, of New York; one of the old school. I admire him as one of the few incorruptible men on the bench; but we have no personal acquaintance. The little man at his side is a queer fish; he used to be tutor to Perry Thorburn, but has burst the chrysalis, I believe, and become private secretary to Thorburn senior." Here Porter nodded informally to Judge Hixon's neighbor, whose glance just then met his. "Name's Quisbrough," he continued as they turned their backs and walked away once more, "and he's as odd as his name. You probably think he looks dull, — so he does, — always has that fagged, sleepy air. But bless you, that's no more than the blur you make on good steel, by breathing. I tell you he's sharp; sharp as a razor."

"I begin to feel interested in these people," said Oliphant. "Somehow it is different here from other places in America: in the others, everybody is in such a hurry, that you need an instantaneous photograph to show you what they are like. They run about so."

"Exactly," threw in Porter. "You have heard of the darkey, haven't you, who found it so hard to make out how many hens he had. He got along very well with counting them all — except one; and that one ran round so, he couldn't count it. That's the way with American society."

Oliphant laughed heartily. "Very likely," he said. "But here in Newport they have more repose: perhaps it's due to the drowsy, peaceful atmosphere."

"Isle of Peace, you know," rejoined his friend: "that's what the Indian name, Aquidneck, means. The 'ile of peace is very emollient; you try it, and see. This all leads back to what I was saying — that you'd better come and bunk with me at my cottage, and settle down for a good season of it. Yes, sir, you'll find the genuine leisure class here. Talk about our having none! — Do you remember what one of our bright girls said to the Englishman who complained that there were no people of leisure in this country —

people who don't do any thing? 'Oh yes,' she said, 'we have those people, but here we call them tramps.' I assure you, the kind of tramps you meet in this place are worth knowing."

"I've a great mind," said Oliphant with slow frankness, "to accept your invitation. Nothing could be better, if we can both keep our independence."

"My dear fellow, I shall insist upon keeping mine; and that leaves you to take care of yourself."

"That's fair, at any rate," the widower agreed. "But, oh!" he added, slightly blushing — "it seems funny to ask — you haven't, in the interval, gone and got married, have you?"

"Not I," answered Porter with decision. "Marriage has its good side; but you make me think of a man I heard of, who got alarmed about an earthquake that was to visit his city; so he sent off his two sons to a country clergyman, to keep *them* safe, any way. Well, after two or three days, the parson, finding the boys lively, wrote to him: 'Please take back your boys, and send on the earthquake.' None of that in mine, thank you! Now tell me when you will come over to the house."

"To-morrow, if that suits you. I must go and look after Mrs. Deering, now."

"All right; but can't you join me, later? There are some men here you ought to know, and they're going to lunch with me at one. Will you take a plate with us?"

"Thanks: if I can."

Hereupon they separated; and Eugene, finding that

Mrs. Deering was ready to go, extricated her from a knot of acquaintances, and escorted her to the spacious arched passage that gives entrance to the grounds. As they drew near the point of emergence on Bellevue Avenue, a high, polished gig stopped at the curb, and the young man who had been driving dismounted, with alacrity.

"Perry Thorburn!" Mrs. Deering whispered, impressively.

As the youth over whom she cast the glamor of that opulent name stood for a moment on the sidewalk, giving some direction to his groom, Oliphant beheld him framed in the archway, with the glare of the outer light upon him. He was a tall, sinewy young fellow, clad in a combination of gray cut with supreme stylishness, that set off his red-tanned face, his long neck and amber-colored hair, in remarkable contrast. His figure, from the great length of the arms and legs, would have been ungainly but for the commanding pose habitual with him. He was not handsome, but neither was he bad-looking; and here again the only half-successful contour of his features was made respectable by the haughty vigor that informed them. Thus much Oliphant was able to observe while young Thorburn stood on the pavement, and as he passed them on his way in, with long strides.

"So that's the heir of his father, is it?" said Eugene. "He looks as if he could spend the money, and if his energies happened to strike in, he might make it, too. You don't know him, I see, personally."

"Dear me, no," said Mrs. Deering. "Confidentially, you understand, he is way beyond us; though I fancy his father buys and sells in Roger's office a good deal. Perhaps I ought to say he is not 'of our set.' I draw the line at the Thorburns, chiefly because I can't draw *them* inside of it."

Then, begging her cousin to come and dine with her that evening, she nodded, got into her village-cart, and drove away.

It was with unusual exhilaration that he returned to the cheerful precinct he had just left. The meeting with Porter had enlivened him; a new zest was making its way into his veins. People were now beginning to leave the spot, and strayed by twos and threes past the rich grass-plots, the beds of diversified coleas, and the heavy stone base of the Clock-Tower; and Oliphant gazed with satisfaction at the fresh, happy faces of the young women amongst them. On gaining the balcony, which was still dotted with scraps of vivid color in the bright morning dresses, and the parasols of "crushed raspberry" that lingered, he at once caught sight of Perry Thorburn, who was just then passing Quisbrough. Perry gave the latter no sort of recognition; a fact which the tutor-secretary took without concern; and, going on farther, was speedily absorbed in conversation with a lady of very striking appearance, in black and yellow, who was obviously much older than he.

I doubt whether Oliphant could have told why, but the sight of the arrogant, attractive young millionaire leaning over and talking with unconcealed earnestness to this handsome woman whom our friend himself did not know, roused in him a blind protest; and forthwith the whole scene before him underwent a change. A moment earlier, it had been agreeably sparkling and satisfactory; now, on the contrary, it became shallow, insincere, and hollow. "They're all on exhibition," he murmured to himself. "It's like the opening scene of a comedy. Bell rings; curtain is up — beginning of the season. In they come, actors and audience; and every one seems to say, 'I'm still on the surface, you see, and I'm as fine as you are. What next?' Bah!"

Taking out his watch, he discovered that it was a quarter after one; and while he was closing it he heard Porter saying: "Ah, there you are, Oliphant! We are just going to lunch."

As they passed up-stairs, Oliphant seemed to hear a voice repeating, "Forty — love; forty — love!"

II.

THE LIFE OF A LETTER.

THE lunch was a pleasant affair, and Porter exhibited himself in a light which brought out his versatile capacity.

Besides himself and his prospective visitor, there were present Atlee and Perry Thorburn; Stillman Ware of Boston (brother of the young lady Oliphant had seen on the balcony); one Admiral Glines of the navy; a retired major in the regular army named Bottick, who seemed to consist chiefly of big. red, bald cranium and iron-gray mustache; and finally a college professor of great scientific repute, who hid his celebrity under a reddish beard, an excellent double-breasted coat, and (on entering the room) a tall white hat, which made him look like a rather solid butterfly of fashion.

With these personages Porter conversed in a way which showed that he was master of their various interests; or could at least convince them that he was. To Glines he talked about torpedoes and the decline of the navy; to Major Bottick, of the war in Egypt, varied by ancient club-gossip redolent of stale tobacco smoke. Thorburn he engaged on matters connected with polo and yachting; the length of water-line in different boats; their owners, cost, and vicissitudes in sundry races. With Ware, again, he deftly assumed the cultivated tone, mingling society and house-decoration with data about rare editions of books.

As they took their places, "You know," he said, quoting from some dead-and-gone society verse, "'Vitellius's feasts cost a million;' but I'm not Vitellius, and I intend giving you to-day only the last two or three figures of that amount."

Nevertheless, so far as it went the repast was delicious, and every one was pleased. Even young Thorburn was mollified into laying aside his unnecessary hauteur, under the influence of a particular claret called Lagrange, which Porter recommended, and of a cigar rather better than those which the young man usually bought for himself. To inhale his entertainer's lavishness in this way was an enjoyment heightened by the sense of his own superior prudence. Oliphant being placed next to him, they naturally fell into talk; and when the party was breaking up, they again found themselves side by side at one of the windows giving on the Avenue.

"There isn't much driving yet, I suppose," half inquired Eugene.

"Oh, it's beginning," answered the other, carelessly. "I believe there won't be so much as there used to be. At any rate, the people who used to drive don't do it so much now, I'm told."

"The set changes, then," said Eugene. "A new dynasty — is that it?"

Thorburn laughed: he was pleased with the phrase. "If you like to call it so," he said. "I'm one of 'em, whatever it is. *I* drive. Later in the afternoon's the hour, you know."

"This isn't your first season here, is it?" Eugene asked.

"Well, yes, really it is," the young man conceded. He betrayed some hesitation, however, as if to admit the fact reminded him uncomfortably of his youth and newness. "Father only built his house here last fall, you know."

Oliphant liked him the better for showing so easily what he felt; and began to think that this young fellow's lofty mode of carrying himself did him injustice. Then suddenly came back the recollection of that scene on the balcony, where the sight of Thorburn and the lady in black and yellow had affected him so curiously; and he was taken with a desire to ask who she was. But this of course could not be done, and he had besides, as he thought, asked questions enough.

Just at this moment they heard a peculiar sharp jingling in the street, which attracted their attention. Perry looked out rather eagerly, Oliphant thought, as if he had been waiting for the sound, or at least recognized it; and as Oliphant's own eyes turned in the same direction, there passed swiftly by a light barouche, properly manned with a liveried driver and groom, and drawn by small, strong horses, bearing at the front of their harness a close-linked steel chain, that churned forth with rapid motion the metallic signal which the two men had heard. In the carriage was seated the identical lady who had just been occupying Oliphant's thoughts. She was of small but not diminutive figure; in a certain way beautiful, or perhaps I ought to say fine, without having much color in her cheeks or any splendor of physical endowment that at once overpowered the eye; above all, she gave an impression of delicate energy, of a something unusual without being obtrusive, and of compact completeness. This it was which made her appearance striking, as I have said it was, when Oliphant had first seen her. She still wore her dress of black, sparingly touched with yellow in one or two places, and a small black bonnet in which a single narrow golden band likewise appeared. Whether she saw the two gentlemen who were looking at her, I cannot say. She was out of sight again, in a flash; gone like some wonderful kind of bird that had been startled out of her covert and had taken a quick flight into other shelter. That was the effect on Oliphant: the carriage and pair dissolved, as it were, and he could think of nothing, for an instant, except the sable form and the dash of gold that had swept by him.

"Who is that lady?" he now asked, easily enough. "I've noticed her before." As he spoke, the jangling of the horses' chain was still heard faintly, and chimed in with an emphasis bizarre and semi-barbaric.

"A Mrs. Gifford," said Thorburn. "Very much of a favorite here, and deserves it, too. She's a bright woman."

"Ah, she's married," Oliphant rejoined, reflectively. "I had an idea she was in mourning."

"Mourning? I should smile! Not exactly. Didn't you see the yellow in her dress?"

"Yes, yes; so there was. I noticed it especially, too." And Oliphant was surprised to find that the black garb, and perhaps something in the general appearance of the wearer, had neutralized the meaning of that vivid color.

"She's a widow, though," added Thorburn, as if he had enjoyed holding the fact in reserve.

"Oh," said Eugene, a little coolly, beginning to move away. He was not quite pleased with himself, on finding that this information revived his interest. "From New York?" he inquired.

"No; Baltimore. She spends part of the winter in Washington, and comes here in the summer."

Oliphant now went back to Porter; they all took their hats for departure; and he was soon on his way to his hotel, alone. The rest of the afternoon was occupied with sundry idle employments, during which he gave little thought to the various persons who had come into his field of experience since the morning; but he was destined to hear more of Mrs. Gifford, and to make a discovery which should give her a fixed and unique place in his reflections.

Putting on his evening dress, he proceeded to his cousin's, and there met Atlee, who was to dine with them. For some cause, the presence of this young man was by no means pleasant to Oliphant: he wondered whether Roger Deering were aware how it looked, that his wife should be accepting Atlee's devotion. True, it was the devotion of an image, a stuffed doll.

But possibly, if Roger had to choose, he would prefer to have the appearance of a fashionable flirtation sustained by something of more dignity than a doll. Atlee was in the small parlor with Mrs. Deering and her two children, — a boy of eleven, and a little daughter scarcely three; they made a very domestic group.

"And how do you like Newport, Clarence?" Eugene asked the boy, assuming a cousinly air.

"First rate," said Clarence, with his hands in his pockets. "I want to go to the Casino hop to-night."

"What, you?" inquired his mature friend, in astonishment. "You're too young."

"No I ain't, either," declared the boy. "Everybody goes; but the best people take the lead. I've heard 'em say that. Ain't we the best?"

"Clarence," said his mother, "you mustn't talk in that way."

"Well, I don't care," he remarked. "I know what they want is young people, to dance. I know how to dance: haven't I been to dancing-school? If papa was here, he'd let me go. Now Mr. Oliphant, you tell mamma to let me. Mr. Atlee ain't any good that way, for all he comes here so much."

"Clarence," his mother repeated, "I'm ashamed of you! If you go on so, I shan't let you come in to dessert."

Atlee, who was some six feet distant from the object of disturbance, affixed his eye-glass, and regarded Clarence painfully; while the boy, in spite of his valiant attitude, gave symptoms of crying.

"Come here," said Eugene, engagingly. "I've got

something to show you." He had, in fact, provided himself with a little present. It was an ivory puzzle-box, of such dimensions that it could be carried on the watch-chain which he had noticed that his young cousin wore. Clarence was at first much interested, but Oliphant soon perceived that he had miscalculated the precocious child's capacity. "Watch-chains ain't in fashion now, you know," Clarence confided to him in undertone. "They wear fobs. Hullo," he continued, examining Oliphant's waistcoat, "*you* haven't got any fob! Why, Steve Richards has got one, and he ain't any bigger than I am; and he's got lots of other things, too. He's got a toy engine, and a real rifle, and a bicycle, and — I don't see why it is! We're just as good as the others, but some fellow always has more things than I do."

Oliphant was amused, and slightly disgusted; but just at that juncture, dinner was announced, and the children were dismissed. Yet even in the brief moment of their leave-taking Mrs. Deering's preference for her little daughter Effie was plainly revealed: she detached herself from the clinging baby arms and the gold-haired face, with a tender, pathetic reluctance.

At the table, some allusion was made to young Thorburn, and Oliphant was prompted to say. "By the way, he seems to be a good deal interested in that Mrs. Gifford whom I saw at the Casino this morning. Do you know her?"

"Oh, yes," said Mary Deering, "I know her. But I don't think young Mr. Thorburn's interest lies especially in that direction."

"Is that because you know that it takes some other direction?" he asked.

"I can't say positively," his cousin answered. "But it's generally supposed that, if he has any inclination of that sort, it is towards Miss Hobart, of New York, you know; Josephine Hobart. You haven't seen her, have you? Well, she's quite the accepted belle, at home; though, for particular reasons, she doesn't flourish so much here at Newport. Don't you think I'm right about Perry Thorburn and Josephine, Mr. Atlee?"

The young man appealed to gave an exceedingly slow and eminently Britannic assent.

Eugene, however, was hardly convinced. "There is something familiar," he resumed, "about that name of Gifford. It's not uncommon, of course; but it's really a New England name. How does it happen that she hails from Baltimore?"

"I believe," said Mrs. Deering, "that her husband *was* a New Englander, and came from your region, Eugene, — not far from Springfield; though when you come to talk about families, it's quite absurd to ask me. I have enough to do to look after my own, as I guess you saw just before dinner. Still, I *can* tell you this much, that he afterwards moved to Baltimore, and that his first name was Helvetius. I can always remember that."

"I should think you might!" exclaimed Atlee, laying down his fork and allowing a subdued hilarity to distend his mustache. "Helvetius!" he repeated, with condescension. "Most extrawd'n'ry name. I should think you might!" His own name was Gustavus, but he had gradually modified it to "Augustus," and kept even that in the background except on occasions when he thought it would be effective.

"Well," said Oliphant, "I'm not much better off than before. I can't 'place' the name, as they say in the country. And yet" —

In a fit of abstraction, he ceased 'to speak. "I don't think your association with the name amounts to any thing," Mrs. Deering asserted, with such a determined closing of her lively lips that controversy seemed hopeless. "But you may be sure, Eugene, of one thing: Octavia Gifford is a woman perfectly contented as she is. She will never marry again."

"But if that's so," said Atlee, "why is it that she doesn't wear mourning?"

"She doesn't, exactly, it's true," said their hostess. "If you notice, though, you will see that she always dresses in black or white, with just a little of one color scattered in. And then," she continued, turning to Oliphant, "I understand she has a theory that it is not quite truthful to wear black entirely. The way she looks at it is this: 'I'm happy, and I still enjoy a great deal in life, so why should I pretend that I don't, and shut myself up in a dark shroud?' But, really, the reason she holds that opinion is that she was so thoroughly happy in her married life."

"You're sure of that, are you?" inquired her cousin.

"Perfectly. The woman isn't living who looks more on the bright side, so far as that goes, than

Octavia Gifford. Her existence has been so satisfactory to her that, in spite of her great loss, there is a kind of radiance over every thing, in her eyes."

"Fortunate person," murmured Eugene; and then other topics came up, which absorbed them until an unexpected noise at the front door, just as salad was being served, interrupted the conversation.

"There's Roger, I declare!" exclaimed Mrs. Deering, at the sound, and she excused herself, to run out and meet him. She came back, beaming more than ever; and Roger himself followed, — active and semi-preoccupied as usual, with a face that appeared habitually red, either because of haste and heat, or good living, and with hair cut excessively short for summer comfort, from the nape of his neck to the edge of baldness rather far back from his forehead. He did not seem at all disturbed by Atlee's presence.

"How do?" he said cordially to both the visitors, giving his hand to each in succession. "Found I could get away all at once, as I was just explaining to Mary. Things rather dull on the street and likely to stay so the next few days, so I thought I'd run on. Let's have some champagne, Mary."

The wine was sent for, and Clarence burst prematurely into the room. "Oh papa!" he exclaimed; and, after a hearty greeting between them: "May I go to the hop?"

"Hop? No. On general principles, no. All hops excluded — except hop into bed. What party is it?" Mrs. Deering explained. "Oh, go ahead, if you want to," said the father easily. "Let him go and look on, Mary. That's all you could do, you know, Clarence: you're too young to dance there. And you don't catch *me* going. If you want to see me, you've got to stay at home."

So the matter was compromised, finally, by the boy's receiving a glass of champagne and water, and remaining with Deering. "I'll look after him," said the latter good-humoredly, to his wife, "if Atlee and. Eugene will look after you."

Oliphant's vague uneasiness about Atlee had been partially allayed by Roger's sudden arrival; now he was again made uncomfortable by the prospect of taking Mrs. Deering away for an evening of superfluous diversion, just at the instant of her husband's return. But as they chatted and smoked over their coffee, while Mrs. Deering made some preparation for the dance, he consoled himself with the reflection that it was foolish to apply his own secluded standard of conduct, which had never brought about much happiness in his case, to the affairs of the sophisticated circle in which he now stood.

Meanwhile the Casino theatre had been lighted up, and people were slowly assembling in the garnished interior, where the white and gold of the walls and the pale-blue silver-starred panels of the ceiling cast a reflected brilliancy upon the polished floor. The first-comers were of a staid and sober sort, chiefly in dark-hued habiliments; and they collected in the gallery, or seated themselves in the remotest chairs near the lower entrances, with a solemn and expectant hush, very much as if they had arrived at church a long time before service. They were simply spectators, and those who were to furnish the spectacle did not straggle in until after nine. Among these were Mrs. Farley Blazer, Miss Ware and her brother, and young Lord Hawkstane, whom it was supposed that Mrs. Blazer intended to marry to one of her nieces, after he should have had time enough to think he had made up his own mind about it. It was of Lord Hawkstane that the Weekly Eavesdropper had said: "His gentlemanly manner has won him troops of friends;" and in the next paragraph it praised the gentlemanly head-waiter at the Ocean House. Besides these, a member of the cabinet, with his wife and daughters, made his appearance; and a foreign minister as well as a couple of attachés of legation from Washington were pointed out to the solemn people in the galleries, by the more knowing of their associates. Some looked anxiously for Count Fitz-Stuart, of whom they had heard as "the last of the Stuarts;" but he was not seen that evening, reserving himself under some mysterious sense of fitness, with which the half-dollar admission may have had something to do. Mrs. Thorburn came, bringing a judiciously small selection of diamonds. There were other men and women who brought their family names — names of a certain antiquity in Boston or New York, — that gave them a distinction, an imperceptible halo, which the unfortunate on-lookers who did not know them entirely missed seeing. It was on the whole an agreeable, informal company, differing little from the average of cultivated persons elsewhere; notwithstanding which a local paper, the next day, lifting the trump of vulgar fame, declared that "the *élite* was in force, America's best society people being represented by *its* fairest ladies and wealthiest citizens."

When Oliphant came in, he met Dana Sweetser hovering about with a ravished expression of countenance.

"It is simply delightful," said Mr. Sweetser. "You see so many charming friends, with no encumbering obligation. And the beauty! Where can you find at hazard so many attractive women as you see around this room?" As Atlee had assumed the duty of finding Mrs. Deering a chair, the gay old bachelor began pointing out to Eugene the persons whom he ought to observe. "But our quota is not yet full," he wound up. "Before the season is over we expect to draw an Italian Count, a Russian Prince, and"—

"No crowned heads this year?" Oliphant put in.

Sweetser turned upon him a faded reproach, which made him regret his jest. "However, that's not so impossible in the future," resumed the ancient Dana, agile in the recovery of good-humor. "The throne business is so uncertain, nowadays. There's something better than a crowned head to be seen to-night, though. Josephine Hobart is here."

"Indeed?"

"Yes; she has got away from her dreadful old father and is visiting friends in town. Enviable friends!"

"I'm sorry to say I've never seen her," Oliphant remarked.

Mr. Sweetser looked woe-begone. "My dear sir,

you don't know what you've missed! Let me present you."

This offer Eugene contrived to evade, preferring some other approach. Before long he discovered his cousin sitting next to Mrs. Gifford, and was thus precipitated into a speaking acquaintance with the widow.

"Have you ever been in Springfield?" he asked, after a few preliminary nothings.

"No," she said. "But how odd that you should happen to ask! Is that your home?"

"Yes. At least, it was; but I have wandered so much, I can hardly call it that any more. I have been abroad, the last three years."

"Mr. Gifford lived there," said the widow, in the most composed and cheerful way. "But he had entirely moved his interests to Baltimore, before our marriage, and so I never chanced to go to Springfield. Is it a pretty place?"

"'Prettily placed' would describe it better," Oliphant said. But he was thinking that, placid though she was, a certain change had passed over her — like the shadow of a sunny cloud — when she named her husband. There was a finer light in her eye, just for an instant: she looked as if she had been thrilled through with a proud memory, yet one that brought with it a pang. "And you were of Baltimore yourself," he went on. "I know some people there." So they began to make note of their acquaintances, as persons must who have little knowledge of each other.

What they said came fitfully; slender trains of words breaking off suddenly, between which the soft notes of the orchestra swept upon them in delicate waves. Then Mrs. Deering would help them on with a laughing remark; and Oliphant began again. To complete his discouragement, Perry Thorburn strode up, even more overtopping in his dress-coat than he had been that morning, and asked for a dance with Mrs. Gifford, which she granted. At the same moment Mrs. Deering began to waltz with Atlee, and Eugene was left alone. He watched the swift but gentle whirl of the dancers. For a moment every thing before him melted into a tremulous, insubstantial glow; a confusion of gold and white and gaslight and rhythmic motion. It was strange to be in such a spot, with such companionship, while his thoughts were straying off to guess at the happiness so confidently asserted of Mrs. Gifford's past, and to ask whether she had given any more for it than he had devoted without getting a like return. What was the secret of these fates? It reminded him of little Clarence's problem in the distribution of toys; but the question went on recurring like the throb of an endless trouble, a refrain to the lively music now ringing in his ears. At last Mrs. Gifford was beside him again, swept to her place by the breeze of the waltz, which died away the next instant; and the room at once became a solid, bright interior full of polished people; no refrain of destiny audible anywhere in it.

Perry Thorburn went on talking to the widow. Suddenly, "I don't see Miss Hobart," he said.

"That reminds me," Oliphant interposed, addressing her. "Do you know Miss Hobart? I have been so anxious to see her." He had begun to catch the accent of the place.

Mrs. Gifford showed a new interest in him. "Know her? Why, she's staying with me!"

"As an invisible spirit?" he asked, glancing around.

"Luckily, no," was her answer, given with due sparkle of appreciation for his little effort. "I don't see her either, Perry," she continued, to Thorburn. "I've lost her in the waltz. And you know," to Oliphant again, "when Josephine is lost, there are so many to find her — it's quite hopeless for *me*."

"Much more so, then, for me," Oliphant said.

The other two looked in various directions, and finally descried Josephine at the end of the room where she had stopped, with the music, and was detained by a little group of admirers, among them Lord Hawkstane.

"I will go over there," said Thorburn abruptly, after a parenthetical glare at Oliphant.

Eugene wondered if the young man claimed a monopoly of both these ladies.

"It will be like Clever Alice," said Mrs. Gifford. "Everybody who goes to find her will stay."

"I venture to predict that that won't happen in this case," he returned, scattering over his remark a light powder of gallantry which softened the contradiction.

"We shall see," the widow smiled.

Miss Hobart did in fact come back almost immediately, on Thorburn's arm; and as Oliphant stood there he was introduced to her.

"I'm a very poor talker," he declared to her, becoming still more local. "I hardly belong here, for I really have nothing to say."

"That is exactly what will give you a perfect claim," said Miss Hobart. "You will be like the rest, then."

This beginning gave them a half-humorous understanding, from which they went on smoothly. Josephine had spoken quietly, softly; neither in the tone of satire nor in that of earnest. From her manner, she might have been imparting a gentle confidence of some sort. Evidently her power lay in her repose; Oliphant was struck by this. She had large, meditative, dark-gray eyes that moved slowly with a hidden glance sidewise; she appeared to be low-browed, but only because of the breadth of her forehead: altogether she was an embodiment of revery. Oliphant even fancied a guarded sadness in her face; and all this seemed to him very strange in a young woman who drew so much admiration. More and more the thought presented itself that she was the centre of calm in the midst of the whirlpool.

If this were true, the similitude was borne out by the fact that swiftly, surely the idle young men in the neighborhood were drawn closer and closer, and soon were held in a semicircle around her. Eugene felt that he was no match for them, and hastily abandoned the conversation. For a while he stayed near the other two ladies, half-silent and uneasy, disturbed by a restlessness which he was at a loss to account for. Then, finding that Mrs. Deering would not remain much longer and expected to drive home in her carriage, he retreated to a door by the veranda; and, after watching the group until he was thoroughly puzzled to decide whether Thorburn was more interested in the widow or Miss Hobart, he departed.

He had to repack some of his things before removing to Porter's, and it occurred to him to do this to-night; but when he had put on his dressing-gown, an impulse led him into quite a different employment. In a smaller trunk that stood near his bed was a quantity of papers, many of them old letters, which had belonged to his wife. He had brought them hither inconsistently enough, since it was on Mary Deering's advice to sever himself wholly from his past that he had come to Newport. But when he had first looked over his wife's belongings, he had been too much affected and too weary to complete the task; and he fancied that the present summer would be a good time to review what remained, and destroy them. The associations of the day and his musings at the dance inclined him now to take a look at these shrivelled relics. He began humming again: —

> "An' I were as fair as she,
> And she were as kind as I,
> What pair" —

Here he unlocked the box, and threw back the lid. A lingering musty perfume stole up from the mass of old writings.... Somewhere down there, he knew, were the early love-letters. There, too, — he shuddered as he thought of it, — was the equally impassioned but stern and bitter correspondence growing out of a long absence of hers, when she had threatened separation. He hesitated to touch any of these: indeed, he wondered why he had kept them at all. But there was a great tenacity in his temperament, and he had always wished to review his experience as a whole, some day, and solve its unsatisfactoriness; so he had held on to these documents with little care what hands they might fall into, were he to die before disposing of them. The same recklessness on that head had once induced him to set down, partly for relief, partly for analysis, memoranda of the mental anguish through which he was passing, due to the luckless struggle into which his married life had fallen. Upon the little book in which he had entered these records his hand rested first, when he began to examine the contents of the trunk, and he turned a few pages to see what was there. Strange, indefensible, even ghastly seemed the bitter things he found; and for the most part they had lost their meaning; yet he remembered how dreadfully real their meaning had once been — how it had scorched his heart. One paragraph, however, struck him, and renewed the old turmoil. It was this: —

"Do we love each other — Alice and I — or detest? I can't decide. But when we are both hating hardest, we cling to each other most, if only for a better chance to stab. Yes; as some have said, love and hate are the same and merely change their effect — as strong essences may either poison to death, or else poison us out of disease into healthy life."

Oliphant put down the book. "And in spite of every thing," he murmured, "I suppose I loved her! Poor child, when she was laid in her grave . . . O God," he went on, looking upward, as if in communion, "if forgiveness is love, you know whether I loved;

but I do not. I know there was too much weakness and resentment and longing for present happiness in me, to make me deserving in the sight of the Highest." For some time after this he remained inert and silent, unaware of any thought except as it might take the form of penitence and prayer. Then he lifted mechanically one of the packets of folded papers, untied it, and began to read. They proved to be letters written to his wife by various friends, some time before he had even known her; and there was not much in them to interest him. Still, he continued to examine them in a cursory way. Suddenly he gave a start; then he raised his eyebrows and looked closer at the written sheet which he was holding. After this he turned at once to the end, on the other page, for the signature. The ink was timeworn, fatigued by its long waiting, but scarcely dimmed. The name stood out clearly: "Helvetius Gifford." Oliphant was sure he had never seen this paper before; but there, pressed upon it with mute emphasis, was the name which he had heard but a few hours since as that of Mrs. Gifford's husband!

Going back, he read the whole from the beginning; and now his eyes were lifted quietly from its lamp-lit surface to the glassy squares of his window. He at length became aware that the dying moon had cast a strange ashen light over the sky. But why had he never heard of this letter before? Why had his wife never told him of the matter? It had been addressed to her, these long years ago, by Helvetius Gifford, and contained an offer of marriage from him, couched in terms of adoration the sincerity of which was unmistakable; words that looked cold and rigid now, in their parallel inky lines — but only as lava looks black when it is cooled, showing none the less where once the fire of its life flowed burning away, into the unseen.

III.

MRS. BLAZER'S DINNER.

PORTER had not shown himself at the Casino dance, his calibre requiring entertainments of greater weight. But he sent his dog-cart to the hotel, next morning, to transfer Oliphant to the villa.

"You look tired," he observed solicitously, on his guest's arrival.

"I'm all right," said Eugene. "I was up rather late. But what a cosey place you've got here!"

"Yes; it does well enough for me. Not mine, you know; merely taken it for the season." Porter was addicted to brevity of speech. "Belongs to a man named Craig. He lives here in winter, but during the summer he crawls off into a boarding-house and lets the cottage. Rent keeps him in funds for the rest of the year, you see. Guess he put most of his money into this shebang, for he seems hard up. His son has to play the organ in one of the churches here, to eke things out. Quite a genius by the way, that young fellow. Justin they call him. You fond of music?"

"Exceedingly."

"Well, I'll get him to come and play for you; piano goes with house. I furnish a good many things, though, including turn-outs. Come, I'll show you your room."

The house was an attractive one, placed near the old Green End Road, which now — with the sham elegance of a parvenu taste — has been rechristened Buena Vista Street. It was supposed to be in the style of Queen Anne; but had that virtuous matron made a progress in its direction, it may be doubted whether she would have recognized it as a leal subject of her reign in art. The deep brown of its exterior more naturally suggested the domestic inspiration of pumpkin pie. But the room to which Raish Porter conducted his guest was quite to Oliphant's taste, and was provided with a sheltered ombra where, in the midst of flowering plants, one could inhale the fresh air and gaze upon the green water in front of Easton's Beach, and the gently mounded pastures farther off, which, as Oliphant knew of old, rolled away into the sheltered vale of Paradise. On those slopes rose a squat, comfortable-looking gray wind-mill, past which a delicate fog was beginning to float in from the ocean, spreading its ghostly influence over the land.

"Now at last I feel that I'm in Newport!" Oliphant exclaimed, with satisfaction.

"Well, my boy, make yourself at home. This afternoon, if you like, I'll take you the long drive. Do as you please — independence compact, you know. I've put you down at both the clubs; convenient. If you want any thing, ring that bell. And oh, by the way," he added, looking around the door, which he had already opened, to go out, "there's a little wagon entirely for your own use. Any time you want it, just tell James."

Without giving his friend time to thank him, he disappeared.

When Oliphant went down stairs, a few moments later, Porter was nowhere to be seen. He looked out of the window; the fog, he saw, had increased. "This is devilish queer," he said to himself. "Where can Porter be?" It seemed to him that his host must have vanished into the fog, and he allowed himself to fancy that perhaps he might not return.

He rang the bell. "Do you know," he asked of the servant, "whether Mr. Porter is in?"

"No, sir, he's not in," said James. "He went out a few moments ago."

"Do you expect him in presently?"

"Can't say, sir."

There came over Oliphant an uncomfortable sense of being a prisoner, and he said to the servant who still waited: "I think I shall go down to the club — the old club; not the Casino. If Mr. Porter comes in, will you tell him that I shall be back to lunch?"

He escaped, and was ridiculously glad to be in the free air once more. He was conscious that the old club, the Newport Reading-Room, was the conservative stronghold, and for this reason he took his way thither, instead of to the Casino. It occurred to him that he had been a trifle rash in accepting Porter's hospitality without ascertaining more about his present status.

At the club, which was nearly untenanted, he tried

to read the newspapers; but the letter which he had discovered the night before kept coming into his mind. What was he to do with it? That was the vexatious point, for apparently there was nothing to be done. One might say that, in an honorable sense, the document belonged to Mrs. Gifford as much as to himself; that she ought to take it and dispose of it in her own way. Yet it would never do to give it to her. No; that was decided: she must not know of it, on any account. He would burn it. Here again he was obliged to ask himself whether he had any right to do so; and he could not be sure that he had. Throwing down the newspaper, he saw Roger Deering, who had just entered the room, standing in front of him.

They dropped into a slow dialogue, and Porter became the subject.

"Yes, I'm staying with him," said Eugene. "But this sudden prosperity of his rather bewilders me. The last time I knew of him he was merely travelling agent of the Magawisca Manufacturing Company. He tells me now that he's launched out for himself; and he appears to be opulent. It's a great change, seems to me."

"So it is," Roger assented. "But I suppose he's entitled to it. He developed a great head for business, and some people think he is a remarkable financier. He certainly has made some long-sighted operations, and is very successful so far."

"So far, eh? Then you doubt his future?"

Deering answered diplomatically: "Why should I? I know nothing about what he's projecting. Only this,

Eugene: as you're my cousin, I'll warn you that I've sometimes suspected Raish"— he lowered his voice, —" of rather snide transactions; and setting that apart, I know that he is taking great risks."

Eugene smiled. "And, as a stockbroker, you consider that against him?"

"I presume, Eugene," was the reply, "that your head is well settled on the horizontal plane; in other words, level. You're not a lamb. You had your stint of Wall Street some time ago, I take it. But Raish Porter is even more seductive than stock-quotations, and I advise you to keep clear of his schemes."

"Oh, I suppose I shall do that any way," said Oliphant; "but I'm obliged for the hint." He had an inclination to talk to Roger about Atlee. Roger, with his ruddy face, his short hair, his busy, active manner, seemed so honest, that Oliphant's dawning anxiety with regard to the attentions of Atlee became doubly painful. But he really had nothing to go upon, and Roger probably would not thank him for revealing it if he had; so he merely asked a few questions about the Anglicized young man. Except for his foreign nonsense, Roger thought him one of the best of fellows, and showed perfect confidence in him. Confidence, it struck Eugene, was the broker's strongest trait; confidence in himself, in his wife, in Atlee, combined with a confidence that he knew the ways of the world, and did not trust anybody too much. Why wouldn't it be a good idea to get his advice regarding the letter? Accordingly, Eugene put the case to him as a supposititious one.

"What would I do?" said Roger in reply, casting up the pros and cons with his chin in the air. "Well, that depends on how much you are acquainted with the lady. However, I should say there is no doubt she ought to have or at least see the letter, some time. It's the square thing. When you know her better, say; or perhaps Mary could help you."

"Oh no; no. Don't say a word to Mary. Please keep the whole thing strictly to yourself. I'll wait and see."

"All right."

Going back to the cottage, Eugene lunched alone, Raish still not having returned; and when at last the latter made his appearance, it was time for the drive. "By the way," said Raish, "I met Mrs. Blazer, and she wants us both to dine with her on Friday."

"She's very kind; but I don't know her yet, you remember."

"Oh, I'll arrange that. I shall present you to-morrow. There will be some interesting people at the dinner; Count Fitz-Stuart, and Lord Hawkstane, and Vivian Ware,"—Oliphant continued to look dubious, —"and that fascinating woman, Mrs. Gifford," Raish concluded.

"Ah, she is to be there? I should like to see *her* again."

"And I don't blame you," said his companion, with an off-hand familiarity that somehow grated on Eugene. But they were now spinning along in the dog-cart; and the soft marine air, with the prospect of soon meeting Mrs. Gifford once more, speedily put him into good humor. Porter went on fluently, telling who lived in the various houses, and striking out witticisms from whatever material offered. But when they had passed out on to the ocean road that follows the shore to Bateman's Point and around again to the harbor, his tone changed.

"I tell you, Oliphant," he declared with vehemence, "that life we've left behind us in the town is all a sham. It drops itself down in one of the loveliest regions Nature can show, and just devotes itself to a surfeit of amusement and artifice, to fal-lal and lah-de-dah. I despise it!"

"Why do you come here, then?"

"Why do *you*, my dear fellow? We must be 'of our time,' you know." And he continued to talk in a strain of capacious dissatisfaction; satirizing the superficial republicanism of American institutions, and declaring with solid cheerfulness that the present state of things must eventually be swept away and a new civilization be built up above the ruins. But as they drew near the outer streets again, on the homeward stretch, he subsided into contented acceptance of the hollow present, and was careful to show Oliphant where Mrs. Gifford lived. It was a house with timbers let into the walls, and raised its high-piled gables showily above the trees on a hill to the west of the polo-grounds, commanding the harbor and Narragansett Bay. "They call it High Lawn," Porter said.

The fog had continued to hang about the island, and it increased at nightfall; so that when Oliphant repaired to his room to sleep, he was glad to see a cheerful fire on the modern-antique hearth. The winking flames reminded him of his first design of burning Gifford's letter. Mustering his resolution, he took the paper out of its repository and went straight to the fire with it, intending to drop it upon the blazing wood; but at the last moment his doubts returned, and he concluded to wait. There was a force in it, a something approaching personality, which he could not overcome; it began to make him nervous; he disliked to put it away again and leave it — as if it might take some action against him unawares, when his back should be turned — for it was no longer a passive thing. Prompted by this unreasoning impression, he put the letter into a safe pocket in his coat, determined thereafter to carry it about with him.

At the usual morning assemblage in the Casino, the next day, he was presented to Mrs. Blazer, who made herself agreeable, but wore a pained, abstracted look. He noticed, too, that she constantly, in moments of silence, compressed her upper lip so that it became suddenly creased with fine downward lines, like those of hidden steel springs.

"I'm glad you will come, Friday," she said, relaxing this pressure and smiling at him; but it was a weary smile, — that of a person absorbed in schemes, all of which were perhaps not going as she wished. Oliphant had a suspicion that this Social Usurper, like her congeners in the history of thrones, must always remain insecure.

"It is very considerate in you to ask me," he replied, "when you have so many to choose from here, and I am little more than a stranger."

"My dear Mr. Oliphant,"— her use of this address savored of imperial condescension,— "I am delighted to entertain an old friend of Mr. Porter's. Besides, you are not so much a stranger."

"No? How is that?"

"Mr. Sweetser has been telling me that he knows all about you."

"He must be a magician, then."

"Oh no, he's a very simple man; a delightful man, too — Mr. Sweetser. He's like a glass of soda-water, always sparkling."

Oliphant caught sight of him in the distance, at that moment, smirking to some ladies on the balcony. "Yes," he said; "he seems to enjoy life thoroughly. But you make me curious. I should like to hear my history from him, because he'd be sure to give it a new vivacity."

"Ah, that's very well said," Mrs. Blazer declared, showing her large teeth in a heartier smile than before. "But he only said he remembered seeing you, or knowing of you, some years ago in Springfield. Mr. Sweetser can remember a long time back — for a young man."

"I don't think I remember *him*," said Oliphant, reflecting."

"I dare say not; I believe he had known Mrs. Oliphant, when she was Miss Davenant. But I notice your cousin beckoning for you over there: she wants to see you."

"Where?" Oliphant turned, and discovering Mrs. Deering, went to join her.

"I am dying to ask you one question," said that

alert little lady, when she had drawn him apart to a quieter spot. "Is it Mrs. Gifford?"

"*It?* What? And what about her?"

"Why, I mean the letter. Is she the widow you meant, when you told Roger?"

Oliphant was thunderstruck. "Is it possible he mentioned that to you?" he inquired, showing his vexation. "I told him particularly"—

"Oh, never mind that," interrupted Mrs. Deering, good-humoredly. "Of course he tried to keep it to himself, but he was so much interested, he couldn't. And do you know, I guessed right away that it was Mrs. Gifford. Wasn't that 'cute of me!" She gazed up at him with such a saucy triumph, that he was obliged to pocket his annoyance.

"I don't know that it makes any difference to me," he said. "But Mrs. Gifford certainly has some claim. I'm sorry I spoke to Roger, even vaguely."

"You might trust me a *little*," said his cousin, in a tone of injury. "Of course I sha'n't allude to it to any one else, in the faintest way. But I want to know if you're really going to show her that letter."

"Of course not. How can I? Would *you* do such a thing?"

"Decidedly not, unless I wanted to give her a shock and make her unhappy."

"But possibly she knows of the original fact already, even if she never heard of the letter."

Mrs. Deering shook her head. "I doubt if she knows; and even if she did, showing her this old letter would only bring it up in a painful, unnecessary way."

"So I think," he returned. "But as long as you had been told, I thought I'd get your opinion."

"Well, I've given it; but you mustn't consider me as advising," said she, settling her chin with the placidness of sated curiosity.

Oliphant was exasperated at the semi-publicity into which he had allowed his secret to be dragged; but he consoled himself with the fact that husband and wife had flatly contradicted each other's counsel.

The day for the dinner arrived, and at Mrs. Blazer's every thing appeared light, gay, brilliant; but the elegance of her big mirrors, teakwood furniture and huge vases was tarnished by a suspicion that it could not be quite genuine.

"We are just waiting for the Count," said the hostess, while she welcomed Porter and his companion. She had on a dress of cream-colored silk, plaited and draped with the elaboration of a bastioned fortress; and around the tightly drawn space at the bottom was spread, like a victorious ensign, a rich applied Turkish embroidery, full of red and yellow.

The servant announced Count Fitz-Stuart, and Porter whispered to Oliphant, "'Positively the last' of the Stuarts. They don't last especially well, eh?"

In truth, the young Count made no very distinguished figure: slim, habile in form, face the color of an apricot ripened under artificial conditions; insignificant teeth, slightly injured; a general expression of light-hearted readiness for whatever should turn up; all this glazed over with a thin magnificence of manner, somewhat run down from want of exercise.

Among the others present were Vivian Ware and her brother Stillman, Perry Thorburn and Miss Hobart, and the two Misses Blazer. Oliphant was keenly on the lookout for Mrs. Gifford, who greeted him with a smile that was flattering because it seemed to promise that, having seen him once, she was glad to meet him again in a more intimate circle. He crossed over to speak with her.

"I didn't see you at the Casino, to-day," he said.

"No, I go only now and then. And to-day I — I was particularly occupied." She looked down for an instant, and then at him, with an almost girlish anticipation of the surprise she meant to give him. "Where do you suppose I was? The most romantic thing you can imagine!"

"If it's romantic," said Oliphant, "I sha'n't try to guess; for only like knows like."

"I don't know what makes me tell you," Mrs. Gifford proceeded; "I'm sure I don't. Well, I was down at old Trinity Church, listening to the organ — on a week-day, you know."

He thought this a flat conclusion, but exclaimed with fervor, "How singular!"

"Yes," said his new friend; "but that's nothing at all. The great point is the organist."

"Ah? Who is he?"

"A young musical magnificence. Justin Craig is his name."

"Craig? Why, I've heard of him. I'm staying in his father's house, with Mr. Porter. Isn't it the same?"

"Yes, yes," cried Mrs. Gifford, alive with enthusiasm. "Have you met Justin?"

The gaslight appeared to Oliphant to burn several degrees brighter, under the influence of this sudden interest.

"No, I don't know him," he said, reluctantly. "You have a high opinion of his talent, then?"

"You shall see for yourself what it is, Mr. Oliphant. He is coming to play for us here, later in the evening."

"Then that isn't he over there by the window, talking with Miss Hobart?" Oliphant had reference to a tall young man with a palish, elongated face, and vaguely high-bred air, who seemed to be uncomfortable in whatever position he took, and had just shaken himself into a fresh attitude before Josephine.

Mrs. Gifford returned an incredulous gaze. "That! Why, that's Lord Hawkstane; didn't you know? Poor Justin would never be invited here to *dine*."

Oliphant was now taken away for presentation to Miss Blazer, the elder, Ruth by name, with whom he was to go in to dinner. Mrs. Blazer led with Lord Hawkstane, and Count Fitz-Stuart escorted Vivian Ware. The dining-room was a rotunda, and the table was circular, too; so that although Oliphant was placed between Vivian Ware and Ruth Blazer, with Lord Hawkstane and Tilly Blazer opposite, he had a good view of the whole company. There were burning candles in slim brass holders set on small circular mirrors; red and yellow flowers, repeating the tints of Mrs. Blazer's embroidery, abounded; and trails of fern led from the central mass to each plate, softening the glitter of the lights, the brass, the glass, and the flame-colored blossoms.

As the turbot *à la béchamel* followed the Little Neck clams, the Count was heard remarking to Vivian: "But this I do not see, why they call him Little Neck, for this feeshes has not any necks of all."

"Next to none," Oliphant hazarded; whereupon Vivian gave him a merry glance that put value into the wretched pun.

Just then Lord Hawkstane monopolized attention by what he was saying to Miss Tilly Blazer; a young woman, by the way, sagacious and picturesque after her manner, with a cultivated air of silliness, and sleepy-looking eyes and nose. She listened with absorption to his account of the fox-hunt. "Yes, I got the mask," he said. "But all this sort of thing," he continued, in his high-pitched, boyish voice, "is very different to England, you know. Beastly stone walls and all that, don't you know; but then it was awfully jolly w'en we came in at the death. How'ver, on the way, we got to one of those windmills, don't you know, — ha, ha!" — he burst into a watery little laugh — "and the fox ran in there. Yes he did, 'pon my word."

"How mean of him!" sighed Miss Tilly.

"Yes," agreed his lordship, after gulping a glass of Sauterne. "Awfully. It was what you call here 'cussed,' don't you know? 'Pure cussedness.'" And he laughed again with gratification at having proved himself a wit. "He was a nahsty little fox. Well, we had to call the hunt together, you know, and begin again. They beat him out, and then I got in front and had an awfully tight pull with Thorburn, and came in ahead; so I got the mask, you und'stand."

"How perfectly lovely!" Tilly exclaimed. "And the mask is the head, isn't it?"

"Yes."

"It sounds so awfully mysterious, don't you know?" she went on, bringing her manner softly into accord with his. "The mask, and the brush, and pads! How I wish I'd been there."

"Why didn't you come?" Lord Hawkstane asked. "Miss Hobart took the run with us, you know: she was almost in."

"I was afraid of those dreadful leaps," said Tilly. "But I *should* so like to see a mask! Do you have it to keep, all for your own?"

"Oh yes," said the youthful nobleman, dallying with the enjoyment of some unexpressed joke. "I'm not sure, how'ver, that I shall keep it." (Tilly blushed, and exhibited a readiness to be overwhelmed by his kindness.) "Rather a baw, you know: what can one do with those sorts of things?"

"Oh, I should think it would be so *very* interesting to have," Tilly replied, with expectant timidity.

"If you really care for it so much," he began, showing the energy of sudden munificence, "I can let you see it, I dassay."

Mrs. Blazer observed that he here stole a look at Miss Hobart, who was at some distance from him; and the hidden springs in Mrs. Blazer's upper lip began to move nervously, in consequence.

Oliphant made good progress with Vivian Ware, during those intervals when Mrs. Blazer engaged the Count. Miss Ware was unlike most of the young Boston women he had known, in that she quite threw aside the prim reserve usually assigned to them as a characteristic. She had been much about the world, and there was a gay freedom in her manner which even subjected her at times to the charge of being " fast ; " yet there lurked in her tone, in her refined features and soft complexion crowned with golden hair — in her entire presence — an unspoiled sweetness that belonged to the flowering-time of life.

" One of the chief things," he said to her, " when I was last in Newport, was to go to the Fort, on Thursdays. Were you there yesterday ? "

" Bless you, no ! " exclaimed Miss Ware. " It's all out of date, now. Last week I believe just one carriage went. It must have felt like a fossil."

" So do I," he responded. " I see I shall have to remodel myself. How would you advise beginning ? Buy a white hat ? "

" If you do that," said Vivian, " you are lost. Black is *de rigeur*, this summer. And then, you must wear little pointed shoes with cloth down the front."

" Why ? "

" Because you must. It's supposed to be the latest English wrinkle."

" How is it with our friend the lord, opposite ? Does he get himself up that way ? "

" Oh, no ; he can wear any thing he likes. He's *real*, you see, and our young men are only imitation. They have to take great pains to pass for even that much: the danger is, they may turn out to be nothing, — not even imitation."

"I'm glad I'm not one of the young men," Oliphant observed, "if that's the way you talk about them."

"And well you may be," said Vivian with sprightly ease. "You'd much better stay as you are."

Meanwhile he had opportunities enough to glance across the flower-strewn board at Mrs. Gifford, and the more he contemplated her the greater was the charm. He retraced the lines of her delicate face; the thin lips, the small mouth and decisive eyebrows. Her brown hair was of the palest that it could be without merging into blonde, but she had chosen to invest it with a slight ornamentation of black lace, which though not sombre gave a hint of widowhood. Her dress was black and white, with a skilful introduction of violet. Quite to the slender throat it came; and the face above, having no strong color, acquired by contrast the remote beauty of warm-toned ivory. To see her smile, toss back her head, drink, look, was to feel a wondrousness about it all, as if an exquisite work of art had suddenly been endowed with life.

As soon as the dinner had worn its way through numerous courses to the cloyment of sweets and coffee, and a respite of smoke had been allowed, Oliphant hastened to rejoin her.

"I begin to think," he commenced, "that you have held out false hopes as to your youthful prodigy, Craig. He doesn't seem to have come."

"No," said Mrs. Gifford, plainly disappointed.

"Mrs. Blazer received a note after we left the dining-room, and it seems he won't be here."

There occurred, instead, a duet by the Misses Blazer; after which he renewed the conversation. But the knowledge of the letter he had discovered hampered him at every step; he was haunted by suspicions that she might know all about that old courtship, and by an uncomfortable fancy that perhaps she knew nothing, in which case he had her at a disadvantage. The temptation to approach the topic indirectly became irresistible.

"We were speaking of Springfield, the other evening," he finally remarked, as if by an accident of thought. "It's strange that I never met Mr. Gifford there. You never heard him speak of me, I suppose?"

"No, I don't remember to have heard him," said Octavia. "What makes you think of that?"

"Well, your name struck me as one that I knew, when I heard it here, on meeting you. Possibly it had come to me in some other way. Perhaps my wife — you see, Mr. Gifford may have been known to her; that is, of course, before we were married."

The reconnaisance was as clumsy as it could well be; but Octavia gave no sign of apprehending his motive. "Your wife?" she repeated, in a hushed tone. "As I told you, I never was in Springfield. What was her name, Mr. Oliphant, before your marriage?"

His voice came lingeringly, as he replied: "Alice Davenant."

"What a beautiful one!" Octavia exclaimed, sincerely, in subdued tones. "It has the ring of poetry in it. Alice Davenant! I'm quite sure, though, that Mr. Gifford did not know her: if he had, I should have remembered his mentioning it."

Oliphant's doubts were thus set at rest. He changed the topic quickly, and availed himself of the first opportunity to ask if he might call upon her.

"Why not?" she replied. "I shall be glad to see you. Are you to remain some time in Newport?"

"Probably through the season," he answered.

"A wise resolve," said she, "in any one. You won't regret it."

I shall not deny that Oliphant attributed to these words a superstitious force which they were not fitted to bear. "That's a good prophecy," he said with vigor, after an instant's revery. "And, since you make it, I think it must be true."

When they had all gone, Mrs. Blazer — left alone with her swan-like nieces, — drew a crumpled note from her pocket. "There!" she cried, to Ruth. "Read that. Read it out loud."

Miss Blazer obeyed. The note was from Justin Craig, declining to be present and returning the check she had sent him. "Allow me to add," it ended, "that I will not debase my art to the amusement of people who, considering me unfit to associate with on equal terms, would have me sit in the same room and exhibit the beauty of something they are unable to appreciate. If you are content with your position, so am I with mine."

"Did you ever hear such an insult!" stormed Mrs.

Farley Blazer, walking swiftly about and fanning herself ferociously. " After Octavia Gifford had been at me to send for him, and I had done it out of pure charity, too! Well, it's just the same, high and low: there's a constant fight with people, even now when I've made them acknowledge me; and it's hardly worth while to do *any* thing. And you there, Tilly, why didn't you go to the meet? Do you know what I've found out? It's another piece of Gifford work, getting Josephine Hobart over here; and I heard Hawkstane saying, just before he left, that he was going to send her a memento of the fox-hunt. Of course it's the mask, which you'd have got for yourself, if you had any vim!"

Saying which, the matron broke into a violence of epithet that, if I were to repeat it, would at once be pronounced unnatural and incredible: therefore we will leave it to be washed away by the tears to which she gave free vent in the midst of her tirade.

But Oliphant, wending back to the supposed Queen Anne cottage, was soothed by his delightful impressions of Octavia Gifford, which like a refreshing autumn rain had begun to lay the dust of his arid past; nor, if he had known of Mrs. Blazer's explosion, could he have guessed how it would affect his own fate.

IV.

SOME IMPORTANT TRIFLES.

"HERE'S a pretty go with young Craig," said Raish to his visitor, the next afternoon; and he related the manner of Justin's refusal, which Mrs. Blazer had been confiding to him. "But the funny part of it," he added, "is the rage she's in. She's formed such a habit, in her long social war, of feeling slighted that she can't be comfortable now without an injury. The case between Craig and her reminds me of the eagle who refused to carry off a fine plump ewe, on the ground that the muttonish creature wouldn't appreciate the honor; and then the ewe went around complaining that the eagle had insulted her."

"Did you tell Mrs. Blazer that?" Oliphant inquired.

"'Gad, no!" Raish exclaimed. "I told Craig, though, when I saw him, a little while ago: thought it would pacify him."

"Well, what does he say?"

"Oh, he's in a sumptuous and haughty frame of mind. It's a pity he behaved so, because this would really have been a good opening for him. But I think I calmed him down a little; and I succeeded, according to promise, in making him consent to come up here and play for you — this evening."

"I'm glad of that," said Oliphant. "This quixotic proceeding of his makes me more anxious than ever to see him."

"The real inside reason why he wouldn't accept Mrs. Blazer's offer," Porter volunteered, "was probably that he has a desperate attachment for Miss Ware, and didn't wish to appear before her in the light of an inferior."

"Good!" rejoined Oliphant. "The interest increases. And the attachment is hopeless, you think?"

"Oh, I don't know that it is. On the face of it, you'd think so: fact, it's ridiculous. Of course I'm with him in sympathy: smash up the cliques, *I* say — except when you're in 'em yourself. 'Down with exclusiveness,' and so forth. Let the genius in humble circumstances marry the swell girl, and all that. As I said to you recently, we must do away with all this old humbug which is re-asserting itself in a country that was made for better things, and start a new order. But for the present the obstacles in Craig's way appear insurmountable; enough so, any way, to make the hopelessness profitable. To him as a musician, you see, despair is just so much stock in trade."

"For heaven's sake," remonstrated the other, "don't put it that way — as if he were carrying on a business in emotions! You make my blood run cold."

Porter laughed indulgently. "It's true, all the same," he said. "Every thing is business, nowadays."

They were smoking their cigars in the cosey bachelor drawing-room, that evening, with black coffee in small Satsuma cups awaiting them on a tray, when Justin Craig made his appearance. Eugene had expected something eccentric; he thought the young man would be tall, gloomy, and in all likelihood long-haired. He was surprised, therefore, to find him so gentle, so inconspicuous, and yet so uncommonly attractive as he proved to be.

"Did you bring any music with you?" he asked.

"Yes," answered Justin, nodding, but with a reserve of humor in his eyes; "I've brought some."

Then, taking his place at the piano, he looked quietly at the keys for a moment, and, before it could well be noticed that he had actually begun, was tracing his way through the first bars of a prelude by Chopin. As the delicate, gradual tones succeeded each other, Oliphant was strangely affected. Something there was so pure and refined in the player's touch, his beginning with this perfectly simple theme showed so true a sensibility, that the world-worn man who listened was carried back to his boyhood, and then far away out of himself into an unknown, sunny-misted region of fancy, where pleasant visions floated round him. All the while, there recurred in the melody, which had about it a great though heart-broken peacefulness, some fine and slow descending notes that brought into his mind imperceptibly the idea of light rain falling.

"Is life so dreary as I have thought?" mused Oliphant, under this spell. "Surely, if it has room for this young fellow, with his heart and head responding to such sweet fantasies, it may yet hold a possibility of genuine happiness for me."

The piece stopped as quietly as it had begun, and he asked what it was. "It's usually called The Raindrop," said Justin. "One of the best of Chopin's things, too. Now I'll give you some of Raff," he continued, plunging at once into a brilliant impromptu.

Porter, after a congenial remark or two, took his leave, on the plea of a business engagement. Thus left alone, the young musician and his new friend enjoyed an hour of rare delight, both in discussing various composers and listening to their productions, as Justin gave them wing upon the keyboard. Justin had a long face; rather a long nose; an expression of natural pride, which yet had nothing domineering about it, and was tempered with natural sweetness. His lips were slightly drawn back at the corners, without being strained; and there was a small hollow just above the chin, caused by the firm jut of the lower lip, so decided that, as the light streamed over him from above, a spot of shadow rested there. His own shadow was thrown behind him upon the dim-papered wall, wavering somewhat with his firm, unexaggerated motion as his hands changed position and grasped from the keys the secret of their harmonies. Altogether, that keen, unusual face, so steady and concentrated in the midst of shifting lights and shadows, with wave on wave of intelligent sound rising up and floating around it, became singularly impressive.

"I'm sorry," said Oliphant at length, when Craig

had stopped to rest, and was lounging in a deep chair with a cigarette in his mouth, — "I'm sorry we couldn't have heard you last night, at Mrs. Blazer's."

Justin jumped up, letting an angry whiff of smoke escape. "I couldn't have played there, Mr. Oliphant, — I couldn't!" he exclaimed. "Why, my fingers would have rebelled, even if *I* had consented. Don't you see how it is? You wouldn't ask me to do such a thing, I should hope. You have too much of the artist in you, for that, even if you have been a business man."

"I'm glad you think so well of me, at any rate," smiled Eugene. "Certainly I appreciate your feeling, but"—

"Oh, 'but,' 'but!'" interrupted the younger man. "There is no 'but' about it. Pardon me; I didn't mean to be rough," he added. "But if you only knew how the snobbishness of this whole place jars on me, and how that incident of last night brings it all back! Oh, it's insufferable, it's miserable! Sham, sham, sham, all around: we're on an island of sham, with the big ocean of reality on every side, which they're all afraid of being drowned in if they once venture off!" He curved his arms out, downward, and swept them round him, to describe this ocean, and went on railing. "Of course," he wound up, "I know there are lovely people here, amiable and cultivated, and so forth; but even they are affected. I see a little of some of them who stay during the winter; but somehow, except with the poor ones, I am made to feel my inferiority. And here is this house — our home — that we have to abandon during the season. Why should I feel humiliated by that fact, if we can't help it? But I am humiliated. There's no sense in it, and it only shows how you can't help breathing in this poison of the plutocracy, that fills the air. I hate every thing and everybody in the place!"

"Including Mrs. Gifford?" inquired Oliphant mildly.

"Ah, Mrs. Gifford! No; I believe she is a good friend. Such a woman as she is! Perfect in herself — standing way off from a fellow, yet so sympathetic. No; I oughtn't to have said everybody; for there's another — one other" — Justin stopped short, relighted his cigarette, which had gone out, and subsided into his chair.

As he sat there, a distant look came into his face; the storminess of his recent mood died away in an expression of great gentleness. Oliphant knew he must be thinking of Vivian Ware.

It was after this that, returning to the piano, Justin played something which startled his auditor by its crisp, clear, bounding individuality. Coming after so many German pieces, it was like the scent of aromatic New England woods and the sound of native speech, on the return from Europe. Oliphant recognized in the music something native and original; and it turned out to be, in fact, Justin's own composition. He no longer hesitated to regard the young man as a promising genius; and he foresaw that to take him in charge and aid him in his professional education might furnish just the sort of motive in life which he himself would like.

Raish did not return until late, when Craig had been gone some time. He appeared in more than good spirits: he was excited,—which with him was rarely the case. His eyes glowed as if from the reflected glare of some crucible seething with combinations that were to yield marvellous results. "You've lost a great pleasure," said his guest. "I wouldn't have missed it, for a good share in the profits I suppose you've been figuring up."

"Do you really mean that?" queried Raish, blandly rubbing his hands.

"Thoroughly."

The shining look passed away from the other man's eyes, which rapidly cooled down under pressure of the will. "My dear fellow," said he, carelessly, seating himself, "a tenth in one of my operations — say my new Orbicular Machinery Company, whose patents you know are going to make it an enormous success — would give, with what you have, a really handsome fortune. But, bah!" he ended impatiently. "I resolved when you came that we shouldn't talk money; and we won't. Don't let me forget again. Have some beer, before bed?"

His hand was on the bell; but Oliphant declined the refreshment. Arrived at his room, he suspected that Porter really wanted to discuss business, and he was glad he had escaped. Assuredly there was something about this man which made it hard to trust him fully; and it was odd that both he and Justin, of whose sincerity Oliphant hadn't a doubt, should have taken the same tone in criticising the Newport spirit. If two men so opposite could agree, there must be something in it, Oliphant thought. This, however, was not what he thought about chiefly, as he sat in his ombra indulging a brief meditation, and watching the pale stars that shot forth their gleams in a silent rhythm. He was brooding over Justin's enamored subjection to Vivian Ware. Wonderful must be the refined passion which drew the young minstrel towards her. Wonderful, too, in a world so full of disappointments, to find a youthful heart — so like millions of other youthful hearts — fired with lofty enthusiasm, lavish in scorn and unreasonableness, and devoutly believing in love! . . . At last, Oliphant's revery settled upon Octavia Gifford, and he even harbored a wish that he also could be young, like Justin.

Two or three days later, Dana Sweetser, bestarched, perfumed, roseate of countenance, and resplendent as to neck-scarf, was making a morning call at Mrs. Blazer's. Something occurred in the conversation which led Mrs. Blazer to tax him with being forgetful. This was touching him in a tender spot, and he became termined to show her that his mind was still young and active. "My dear madam," he exclaimed, "you couldn't make a greater mistake! Accuse me of other faults, if you like, — ah — too great a fondness for the fair sex — he, he! — but don't accuse my memory. Why, it's the easiest thing to give you proofs of its strength." Dana was really on the verge of being incensed: his little thimbleful of soul was tossing with puny indignation. It occurred to him that he might tell her how well he remembered the time when her father was a butcher, — not a very good one, either, — and how her husband had begun in life as the proprietor of a junk-shop. But it did not lie in Dana's composition to do any thing so harsh as that; so he punished her merely by recalling a quantity of dry details about long past trivial events. Mrs. Blazer was beginning to wince under the infliction, when he suddenly struck a new vein. "Oh, and Mr. Oliphant, you know!" said he. "I was telling you I knew about *him*. But I didn't get a chance to mention the oddest thing. What do you suppose?"

"Can't imagine, Mr. Sweetser. What?"

"Why," — Dana laughed, seemingly inclined to prolong the pleasure of imparting, — "his wife, you know, the girl he married" —

"Whom did he marry?" Mrs. Blazer asked, growing curious.

"Alice Davenant, — Miss Davenant, of Springfield. But the joke is this: she had previously jilted Gifford, the husband of Mrs. Gifford the lovely, here. Isn't that singular?"

Mrs. Blazer's eyes glowed. "As a coincidence, yes; very singular. And Octavia hadn't known this Mr. Oliphant, do you suppose, till they met, the other day?"

"No," said Dana; "I believe they were strangers."

"Well, well, upon my life!" Mrs. Blazer exclaimed, smiling with peculiar relish. "Of course they must have known the facts, though," she added, contracting her glance to an evil watchfulness.

"That I can't say," Dana rejoined, as thoroughly

mellowed as if he had taken a glass of wine. "I should think Oliphant must have known; but it wouldn't be so certain that Mrs. Gifford did, you know: would it?" And he cocked his appreciative eye at her, like one competent to get the full value out of such matters, by discussing all the minute possibilities of doubt.

The lady of the smoky white complexion humored him and suited herself, by carrying out this process. "First tell me all the particulars you know," she said, "and then I can form a judgment."

So Dana bubbled on, joyously chattering out the shallowness of his information, with utmost generosity: it was all he had to give, and he gave it. He had vindicated his memory; he had interested Mrs. Blazer.

From what she had gathered, Mrs. Farley Blazer came to the conclusion that Octavia probably knew nothing of that old history; but, for purposes of her own, she assumed just the contrary when she next saw the widow. She could not forgive Octavia for having drawn down a mortification upon her, by urging her to invite Craig to play for hire, and so putting her into a position to be snubbed by the youngster. Still less could she overlook the offence of bringing Josephine Hobart back to Newport, to distract Lord Hawkstane's attention from Tilly. Accordingly, when Octavia came to pay her dinner call, Tilly's aunt found an apt moment for remarking casually, "Oh, my dear, what a queer thing it is that you two should have met here, — you and the man whose wife was an old flame of your husband's!"

Mrs. Gifford showed an amused surprise. "It would

be queer," she said, calmly, "if there were any such man; but there isn't. What put it into your head? Whom do you mean?"

Mrs. Blazer unfolded her meaning; but, to her chagrin, it produced no shock. Octavia persisted in her laughing incredulity, and ridiculed Dana Sweetser's evidence. "You may be sure," she said, "that he has been mixing us up with other people." And before Mrs. Blazer saw clearly how it was done, Octavia brought in another topic, and then took her leave, completely uncrushed.

These things had happened before Eugene, on his way to see Mrs. Gifford, stopped in at his cousin's.

"Have you heard the news?" she immediately asked him.

"Yes; Major Bottick told me at the club," he answered.

Mary Deering's face became blank with astonishment. "Major Bottick!" she exclaimed.

"Certainly; he's up in all these war matters. Of course you mean about the English and the Suez Canal?"

"What have I said about a canal?" inquired Mrs. Deering, aggrieved.

"Oh, then you're thinking of the President's expected visit here?"

"No, indeed," said his cousin, still more reproachfully. "How dull of you! Do you call those things news? What I'm talking about is Lord Hawkstane's engagement."

"Hullo! Isn't he rather 'previous'? Whom is he engaged to?"

"Josephine Hobart."

"Well, that has the approved stamp of news; it's so incredible. Have they announced it?"

"Not yet; but a few of us know it. He sent her the mask that he won at the hunt; had it set in a collar of gold and surrounded with the most magnificent flowers: just think of it! Then he went up yesterday to call, and, as we suppose, offered himself. He's been so puffed-up and vainglorious ever since, that hardly any one can approach him, even to offer a congratulation. So you see there's no doubt of it at all: they're engaged. And it will be an awful blow to Mrs. Farley Blazer!"

"I can hardly believe it yet," said Eugene. "I can't see why Miss Hobart should take him. Have you asked Mrs. Gifford about it?"

"No; I've had no chance. But I intend to."

Oliphant told her that he was about to call upon the widow.

"Oh, do," urged his cousin, "and then tell me what you find out about the engagement. But mind you, don't let her know of that letter."

"No danger," said he. "I have decided *that* point." Before long he broke out, "By the way, speaking of it's being a blow, how about young Thorburn? If you were right in thinking he was in love with Miss Hobart, this will be a bitter thing for him."

"Ah, Eugene," said Mrs. Deering, laying her hand on his arm, "save your compassion. I was mistaken about that: it's Mrs. Gifford that he's after."

"Oh," said Oliphant, amazed at the ease with which

she changed her view. "Being a woman, I suppose you must know. But don't you remember how at the first I thought Mrs. Gifford was his object?"

"Yes, Eugene. It must be that you have a sort of feminine instinct."

"Possibly," he answered, with some dryness. "I am thinking," he then said slowly, "that his courtship of the widow will leave him as badly off as if he had been trying to marry Miss Hobart; provided you are right as to Mrs. Gifford's being so unapproachable. You recall what you said, I suppose."

"Yes."

"It doesn't seem to me, though, that because she was so happy, before, is any reason against her attempting matrimony again. I should say her former experience would work as an argument directly in favor of renewing her happiness with some other worthy person, if she should by accident find one."

"I know," was Mrs. Deering's reply. "That's the way men would look at it. But then — Eugene," she recommenced, with unwonted earnestness, "have you noticed those clear, bright diamonds she always wears in her ears?"

"I think I have, the few times I have seen her."

"Well, they're a kind of symbol," said Mrs. Deering, impressively. "*I* think they're like petrified tears! They don't attract attention, but they're always in sight, as silent emblems of her loss. Yes, yes," she went on — and it was remarkable to Oliphant how his lively and conventional little cousin was aroused and thrilled by her own fantasy, — "they are talismans!

And until a man had got them away, or persuaded her to stop wearing them, it would be no use to attempt winning her." In reaching this climax, nevertheless, Mary Deering, apparently overcome by the absurdity of the notion, burst into a laugh.

"That will do very well as a superstition," said Oliphant, smiling, although her remark had produced no little effect upon him.

She sat there unheeding: one would have supposed she had not heard what he said. She picked away with her needle at some rosy thread which she was stitching into a pattern, and the light from it threw a soft reflection on her face. Can it have been that she had deliberately tried to incite Oliphant to make some advance towards the widow?

I only know that he grew restless. He began to think it was of the highest importance to see Mrs. Gifford immediately, as if something of great moment was to be settled by doing so.

"I must go along," he said, rising. And in half an hour he was at Octavia's door.

V.

A WOMAN'S AGONY.

AT High Lawn, Oliphant was ushered into an apartment so prettily devised that it was like a fair and open countenance.

He was conscious of having made a real advance in his acquaintance with Octavia, merely by stepping into this dwelling-place of hers. The room was finished in holly-wood, with a dead surface, smooth like ivory, but pleasanter, because it still had somewhat of the freshness of a limber growth that had once swayed in the breeze. Panels along the walls were filled in with wine-colored silk, upon which silver thread and vari-colored floss were embroidered in slender lines. There were low seats scattered about, covered with pale tints of this wine hue and with clear sea-green; and the whole place looked above all cosey and inhabited, as if its usual occupant were not afraid of its richness and refinement, or at all subordinated by it, but made herself at home there as in her native element. On a small side-table lay some new worsted-work and a large book, open at the page she had last been reading. The plan of the room was slightly irregular, including near one end a spacious embayed window, the panes of which were set in delicate wood-tracery, where the sunlight was treasured up and some plants grew brightly. Oliphant moved thither, and while he was looking at the gossamer threads of the embroidery on the wall, he heard a light movement, turned, and discovered Mrs. Gifford, who had come into the window-space through an unnoticed doorway. So for a moment she stood there against a vista of lawn slope and trees that led down to the level, shining reaches of the bay; a figure full of brilliancy and gladness, that seemed to concentrate in itself all the charm of the surroundings.

"You see I have come soon," he said, shaking hands. "And is Miss Hobart still with you?"

She had motioned him to a chair, and had taken a place for herself on a sort of huge pale-green cushion which did duty as a seat.

"Yes, Miss Hobart is still here, but she has to excuse herself to-day."

Oliphant wondered whether Josephine's invisibility were due to a rapturous privacy consequent upon her engagement. Just then his eye fell upon the fox's head, of which he had heard so much: encircled by a mass of flowers, it lifted its furry nose from a table near by.

"A little trophy," said Octavia, smiling. "Lord Hawkstane sent it to Josephine. How does it strike you?"

"I think I should like the flowers alone better."

"I'm glad to have you say so," she declared. "It's dreadfully cruel."

"The sport? Yes, it is cruel; and it's empty,— emptier than that poor creature's head."

"Of course you mean the fox's head," observed Octavia, a twinkle of sarcasm in her eyes.

"Of course," he answered, laughing.

"As to the sport," said Octavia, "Josephine followed the hounds, and that part of it doesn't seem so cruel, you know. But having the poor head served up in flowers does strike me as rather savage. Hawkstane got the idea from one of his American friends. He never would have thought of any thing so barbarous himself; but it was suggested to him as the proper way to do things here."

"Possibly," Oliphant contended, "his friend was right. Isn't it the spirit of the place to be idly busy and fill up the time with expensive nonsense?"

"Do you really think so?" she asked.

"I'm not sure that I do," he returned. "I really enjoy this Newport existence. Still, I suspect it of being what I just called the sport — empty. There's an immense amount of occupation: dressing, dining, driving, show. But it becomes a routine, and there doesn't seem to be any good reason for the thing. In fact, I have a radical friend who declares that Newport is wholly un-American, and ought not to exist."

"Ah, that's the trouble with us," Octavia remarked. "There are so many American things that are un-American."

"What's your own opinion?" Oliphant asked.

"Mine? Oh, I glory in Newport! I'm devoted to it. I don't pretend to account for myself, in that; but when you love a place or a person — really love, I mean — you like the faults as well as the virtues, don't you know?"

"And on that basis, if there are no faults, it's just so much deprivation, I suppose," said he, enlarging on her theory. "But I'm afraid I made a mistake in speaking so scornfully of Newport. You will condemn me."

"Not at all. I like candor, though of course it needn't always be put as Justin Craig put his to Mrs. Blazer. What an unfortunate affair, by the way!"

"Yes, conventionally speaking. But don't you find it refreshing sometimes to have people come out with exactly what they feel, even if they are a little crude about it?"

"Indeed, yes." Octavia spoke quickly, and as quickly added: "It depends on who the people are. I like Justin very much: he's so true to himself. But I remember your cousin saying — and how sharp she is! — that it's the same with people as with some of the things we eat. When fish tastes too much like fish, we don't like it, simply because we say it's 'too fishy.' And so it won't do for people to be too much themselves in society: if they are, they're not acceptable — though a slight flavor of individuality is much esteemed. Isn't that clever?"

"Rather so. A certain amount of deceit is necessary."

Octavia sighed, placidly. "At our age, Mr. Oliphant, one comes to recognize that principle."

"Still," Oliphant observed, "there must be exceptions. Now when I meet anybody in whom I'm likely to be interested, I go for clearing away all surface deceits at once: I try to get down to a simple and straightforward understanding as soon as possible."

"That's the best way in those cases," said Octavia. "The danger is, your frankness may be misapprehended."

"Very possibly it may," he returned. "But there's an instinct that tells us when it will be taken amiss. I imagine, in fact I'm pretty confident, that *you*, for instance, would be careful not to misapprehend."

She laughed, greatly at her ease: his admission that he was likely to be interested in her was so ingenuous. "I should try to be careful," she replied.

He recognized the position in which he had placed himself. "There," he said, "you see how, the moment we try to be sincere and direct, we become personal. That's the reason people are so afraid of sincerity: they dread being personal. I had no intention about it, but now I find that I've been trying to get this very point settled between us."

Again Octavia laughed, adding, "It seems to have settled itself." And so, in truth, it had: they were no longer mere acquaintances, but had made a beginning of friendship.

Oliphant now remembered his cousin's injunction to find out something about the engagement. Mentioning it, he asked, "May I offer my congratulations, through you?"

"I haven't been empowered, Mr. Oliphant, to receive them."

"Then the rumor isn't true, I infer."

Octavia saw fit to be mysterious. "If you want to know," she counselled him, "you must go to Josephine herself, or to Lord Hawkstane."

"I can't very well do that," he said.

"It is queer how reports get into circulation," she began. "Something has just come into my mind"— Then she hesitated.

"Some other rumor?" Oliphant queried.

"Yes: a ridiculous one. But it isn't worth mentioning."

He was wondering what it could be, when the maid entered with a letter on her salver. "Beg your pardon, ma'am: the man said it was to be given you right away."

Octavia apologized to her caller and broke the envelop, which bore a glowing gold monogram on one side and a dashing superscription on the other. It was a note from Perry Thorburn, asking her to drive with him that afternoon. "There's no answer at present: I will send one very soon," she said to the maid, and laid the note in its cover on a bracket-shelf.

"Don't let me incommode you," said Oliphant, rising.

"Oh, no. Wait a little. I think you are interested in Justin, and I want to talk with you about him. Perhaps we can get him a chance for a concert which can be made fashionable, and you may be useful in persuading him to it."

Oliphant resumed his place; but she noticed, as she thought, a strange look in his eyes, which had not been there before the arrival of the note. The incident brought Gifford's letter freshly up in his mind. He was imagining how it would be if that letter, instead of the one with the gilt monogram, had just come to her.

"Of course," he said, "I shall be glad to do any thing I can to assist Craig, especially if I please you by it."

"Ah, that is very nice," said the young widow, with almost girlish enjoyment. Nevertheless, they were both thinking of something else than their words indicated. Octavia, for her part, had been growing restless over Mrs. Blazer's assertion of a former attachment between Gifford and Miss Davenant, particularly since a second rumor had come to her ears; and she was anxious to controvert it. This was what really occupied her mind while she spoke so glibly of Craig. "It's very nice," she repeated, inertly, once more becoming aware of that look in Oliphant's eyes. "But you seem to speak in a different tone now. You're not enthusiastic. Are you concealing something unfavorable?"

He tried vainly to shake off the reserve which he knew was creeping over his manner. "About Craig? No; nothing."

"At any rate," said Octavia, with unconcern, "I have no right to cross-examine you. We were just talking," she went on, "about frankness. If you're not keeping any thing back, I confess that I *am*, though it has nothing to do with Justin. That rumor I mentioned just now — that is what I'm holding in reserve; but I think I must tell you about it. You will see that it's not quite pleasant to speak of; but I am annoyed by it, and want your help."

"Well, then, there's that much of good in it," Oliphant answered, more at ease.

She paused an instant; then resumed, in a tone of wonderful gentleness: "You asked lately, Mr. Oliphant, if I had known your wife's name."

A chill passed through him. What was coming? What had she discovered? He merely bent his head assentingly, and she continued: "It was a coincidence that you should have asked me that question, because of something else that came up soon afterwards."

"Indeed?" he said, his apprehensiveness increasing.

Octavia betrayed embarrassment. "Yes; it was hinted to me that Mr. Gifford had known Miss Davenant and had been an admirer of hers — a devoted admirer, in fact, before he and I had met." Here she smiled, perhaps from nervousness; but Oliphant remained gravely silent, waiting to hear more. "Of course," she added, "as Mr. Gifford never had spoken to me of her, the notion seemed improbable; but now there has been a second rumor, and this time it is said that you know all about the history. I hope you will pardon me for mentioning it: you can guess that I never would do so unless I thought there was a duty involved. The gossips have no right to be inventing tales about those two who have gone. I thought you ought to know how your name is being used; and really it is for both our interests to stop such idle talk, don't you think?"

The gentleness in her voice had insensibly increased, until the words flowed like the notes of distant music: the tone was subdued, verging upon tremulousness. Both she who spoke and he who listened were thrilled by one chord of memories solemn and sweet, though to Oliphant it brought an after-tone of endless repining.

"Who would have thought," he mused aloud, not answering her questions at once, "that we who did not know of one another's existence, a few days ago, should so soon be speaking of things that lie nearest to us? I think it shows that there ought to be confidence between us. And now in regard to your question, Mrs. Gifford, — I quite agree that our interests coincide; we want to stop the chatterers. I suggest that the best way is to ignore them."

"That's easily said," Octavia objected; "but I can't do it unless you help me. You see, they are quoting you."

She gazed at him with a certain innocent confidence, against which a vague inquiry contended. It was evident to Oliphant that she counted upon him to deny the rumor, and so assist her to a triumph; and it gave him a poignant regret that he could not do this.

"What have you heard as to my knowledge?" he inquired, still dallying.

"It's hardly worth while to go into that," she replied, "unless you really know something. But tell me; there is no truth in the report, is there?"

Oliphant was in a pitiable dilemma. "Are you not troubling yourself needlessly?" he said, in perplexity. "I am not responsible for all this. If you compel me, I suppose I must admit that there is ground for what has been said; but it is wiser to let it rest."

"That is impossible," declared Octavia, becoming imperious. "I want to put the whole thing down; and, in the form which it has taken, that can be done only by positive denial."

"I see that my doctrine of candor is being put to a terrible test," he interposed, attempting to take a light tone, although really in consternation.

"Mr. Oliphant," said she, "I must know whatever you have to tell me. Is it not my right?"

"Undoubtedly, if you choose to assert it. But, after all, I have little to tell."

"You have no disproof" — she hesitated — "or proof?"

"I have a letter; that's all."

Octavia did not respond. She withdrew into herself; her eyes sank. Oliphant fancied that she shuddered.

"A letter from Mr. Gifford?" she then asked, looking straight at him.

"Yes; a letter to my wife, before she became my wife." He met her eyes, and tried to appear as if he attached slight importance to his statement.

"Ah," she scarcely more than whispered, "it was something of that sort that I heard."

"You heard of the letter, too!" he cried, hotly. "Then some one must have been guilty of treachery."

"What else could you expect, if you told any one?" the widow inquired, as icy as he was the opposite. But her eyes were not cold: their luminous depths were softened by a look of tender pleading.

"I have not told. I beg you to believe" —

"I will believe nothing that you say I ought not," she interrupted with dignity.

"Very well. What has become known is due to an accident. I cannot even comprehend how you have been spoken to as you have." Oliphant rose, and, moving a pace or two, drew his gloves impatiently through one hand, knitting his brows in bewilderment and vexation. "It's wrong, it's unfair," he muttered, "that this should be brought upon me."

Octavia changed her mood as instinctively as one might in improvising upon a sympathetic instrument. "Oh, well, we ought not to distress ourselves," she said; though Oliphant knew perfectly well that she was suffering keenly. "Why shouldn't Mr. Gifford have written to Miss Davenant, if he pleased? I dare say it quite passed out of his mind afterwards; and that is what makes it seem so odd that we should only now be discovering their acquaintance. The whole thing is simple enough."

"Certainly; quite simple," Oliphant rejoined, grasping at a chance of escape that promised so well. He was dumbfounded by the rapid and conflicting turns through which he was being led, but made a manful effort to keep his balance. "I'm glad you don't give it too much consequence," he ended.

"Only I shall want to see the letter, you know," she suddenly reminded him, with a gracious smile, but looking very determined. Her head was bent a trifle sidewise, and she gave him a long, steady glance, which was like a sharpshooter's in taking aim.

Then Oliphant recognized that it would be futile to

hold out any longer. "It shall be as you like," he said. "Only let me say that no one else has read the letter."

"So much the better. Have you it here?"

"In Newport? Yes: I can send it to you." He could not face the ordeal of handing it to her in person.

"Thanks. Very soon, too, I hope. Could you let me have it to-day? You will understand my eagerness to see any thing that my husband wrote."

"Oh, yes, I understand." He pitied her from the bottom of his heart, as he stood there looking down at her. Did she see the compassion in his eyes, I wonder? Why could she not comprehend his reluctance to give her pain; and why could she not let him judge what was best for her peace of mind?

What a beautiful picture of grace and contentment she made in that charming room, with its embroideries and sunlight and delicate colors! What a picture of a smiling and unruffled life her face suggested! And here was Oliphant compelled to bring disturbance and disaster into the scene, through no fault of his own; knowing well that when he next beheld her there would be a change — that things could not remain the same after she should have seen the letter. "You shall have it in half an hour," he said. Then, instead of going at once, he paused. "I hope you will not misjudge me in this matter. I can explain more, perhaps, by and by. But would you mind letting me know who it was that brought you the reports?"

"I'd rather not, now, Mr. Oliphant. Let us leave

that till afterwards, too; but I will try to think that you are not to blame."

And so, with the friendly smile she gave him in parting, he made a barren effort to solace himself as he drove away. Wondering how Mary Deering could have been so reckless as to circulate the story of the letter — for he supposed that it must have come from her — he mechanically put his hand into the inner pocket where he had been carrying the vexatious little paper burden; but it was no longer there! Where to begin the search for it he could not decide; but as he was near Mrs. Deering's, he ordered the coachman to stop at her house, resolving at least to investigate her conduct. He re-appeared in the small parlor in a stormy mood; questioning and accusing his cousin and denouncing people in general. She persisted in asserting her innocence; and he went his way again within five minutes, a dim hope that he might have left the letter in another coat lending haste to his movements. His anxiety increased every instant, until he reached the Queen Anne cottage and, dashing upstairs, entered his room. There, surely enough, he found the momentous letter slumbering in a coat which he had not had on for two days. Not until he had enclosed it and sent it away by a paid messenger did the ugly surmise enter his mind that his occult and ubiquitous host, Raish, might have played the spy, coming upon this document during some one of his own absences from the room.

When Octavia received the long envelope, she was still in her pretty holly-wood drawing-room. Not a word of comment accompanied the enclosure, and, tearing off the cover, she instantly scanned the contents.

Unnoticed, the yellow sheet fell to the floor, when she had read the last words. For whatever purpose circumstance and the power above circumstance had preserved it, it had done its work.

Octavia remained passive for some time in her chair, gazing blankly before her. When she finally stirred, it was as a somnambulist might have done: she moved from one part of the room to another, unconsciously, with hands knotted together and knuckles pressed backward against her smooth forehead. Heat at its utmost becomes white, like numb, chill snow: was it by a similar transformation that the burning agony in her brain now seemed not to burn at all, but to be freezing her into insensibility? A curious effect, this. She began to wonder at it; she had a wild inclination to laugh; but with that desire a clearer sense of her misery awoke. "What right had he to send me this?" she moaned. "What have I done, to be so crushed? — and he a mere acquaintance, a stranger! It's unbearable; yes, it's a crime! And I shall never, never" — her voice sank to a whisper more ominous than even the dreary wail that had preceded — "never forgive it."

Ah, if she could have wept then! But the fountains of her life were choked; a parched desert seemed to spread itself all around her and within.

Turning away, she strayed slowly down the room again; this time looking closely at one object after another: at the opaline glass of the chandelier, at a rotund porcelain Buddha contemplating with his fat face a Spanish *navaja* six times his own length, and at the fox's head, which she could almost believe returned a sardonic gleam of intelligence. Every thing was strange, as if she had never been in the room before. Finally, she came to the table where her fancy-work and the open book lay. The volume was a sumptuous one, suggesting leisure, elegance, peace; and her eye rested on these words: —

"The Heart is a garden, and youth is its Spring, and Hope is its sunshine, and Love is a thorny plant that springs up and bears one bright blossom that has nothing like it in all the world."

"Oh no, no, no!" she said aloud, not with protest, but with scorn. "That isn't true. It isn't a thorny plant, but only a weak and miserable weed, with a black, deadly blossom. The 'heart is a garden,' you say — but what if there's nothing but grave-dust in the garden? Oh, why do they write so of love? Why should we be fooled with this sort of thing, and be brought up on it, when it's all a lie!"

Again her hands were locked; she sank upon a couch; she was shaken by her rage against fate, as the air is made to quiver with visible heat in the furnace of summer.

Every thing on which she had built her happiest faiths was swept away at one blow. She had believed that her husband had never loved any one before; but she could never again be sure that he had really loved her at all. Perhaps she had been to him only the solace of a concealed disappointment. Her own pride was wounded: she was angry at her husband, impalpable shade though he was, because he had hidden this thing, had left her to be humiliated and to question where his heart's deepest fealty had been given. Yet at the same moment her pride on his behalf was stirred up against Oliphant, because he knew of Gifford's rejection by another woman.

"I shall go mad, if I think of it!" she groaned. A spasm of unearthly jealousy seized her: Gifford had passed away to another world, and Alice Oliphant had gone thither, also. "He is mine!" Octavia muttered passionately, with a force as if she were calling to some one far away. "We were to meet there; because the fable is that love is everlasting. Have *they* met instead?" And as the shadow of her love and wrath loomed up distorted on the mist that veils all life beyond us, she trembled for her sanity; the prospect grew so dark, she began so to doubt of heaven itself.

In the midst of this horrible turmoil, she rose, crossed the floor, and mechanically picked up the fallen letter. That petty precaution brought her back to self-control.

She was hungry for action. Something definite must be done. She must find a relief, a compensation, for the strain she had undergone. Should it take the form of revenge? A plan flitted through her brain, and she adopted it instantly; but, whatever it was, the first steps did not suggest any thing like danger.

Ringing the bell for her maid, "Take away that fox's head," she commanded, "and don't let me see it again.

And come back immediately: I shall have a note to send."

Seated at her writing-table in the embayed window, she dashed off not one note, but two. The first was to Perry Thorburn, accepting his invitation to drive, two hours later. "Mr. Oliphant shall see, at any rate, that I'm not crushed," she declared aloud. The second note consisted of a few lines to Oliphant himself, thanking him for his promptness in gratifying her wish, and saying that, if he would call soon, she would like to speak with him further.

Thereupon she consulted the lozenge-shaped mirror that hung in velvet on the wall; and the mirror gallantly sustained her: instead of the lines of distress which had so recently shown in her face, it revealed a triumphant energy. No; in all this there was nothing to alarm a possible observer. Yet any one who knew Octavia well might have thought her too determined to be safe; and there was a hard glitter about those symbols of her widowhood, the diamonds at her ears.

VI.

DEWDROPS AND DIAMONDS.

THE weather was delicious; brilliant yet soft, and full of that vague, lulling enchantment which is the peculiar virtue of the Newport air. The sun shone, but not in a downright, uncultured way, such as might be obnoxious to polite sensibilities: you were conscious of it rather as a diffused exhalation of pale golden mist, a celestial form of the grosser golden mist that was floating about in the minds of the people who moved under its radiance, in the holiday part of the town. I have no doubt the wealthy ones among them were gratified that the sun so well understood its place and behaved with such very proper deference; others, whose slender purses enabled them only to cling to the edge of the show, dilated their chests and absolutely enjoyed a passing illusion that they were rich. It was one of those days when a south-west breeze, streaming over the island in a steady succession of bluff gusts makes you feel as if you were standing on a quarter-deck — a deck neatly carpeted with verdant lawns, embowered in trees, and thickly encumbered with villas, a few of which are more like small palaces. Yes, the wind pats your face in a vigorous, companionable manner that flatters you with the idea that you are an old salt, and know all about it, and can stand any amount of exposure — as long as the grass is dry and your nice clothes are not spoiled, and your pleasant club is near at hand. You even murmur to yourself something about "The Bay of Biscay, O;" and then you think of distant places, all the balmy and romantic coasts and islands from which this breeze has come; and the name of far Cathay forms itself lazily on your lips. At least, this was the case with Oliphant, when he came out into the air again, to fulfil an engagement he had made. He had accepted a maternal sort of invitation from Mrs. Farley Blazer, to drive with her. This poor old ogress was rather lonely in her splendor; and as the girls were driving with other people that day, she wanted a companion. Besides, she may have had some faint design of marrying Oliphant to the elder niece, if nothing better could be done. Her foreign policy had had in view alliances with England and France, or possibly Italy: if such an international concert could be established, her own position would be made more secure. But she was discouraged, just now, as to Tilly's capturing Lord Hawkstane, unless the reported engagement with Miss Hobart should come to nothing; and there was beginning to be some danger that Ruth would not get married at all; in which event even so humble a match as Oliphant might be worth considering. Of course he had no suspicion of such an absurdity; and as I have said, he thought of far Cathay, while the breeze wafted aside his troubled mood regarding Octavia. He surrendered himself to the scented indolence and poppied ease of Newport, as being more easily attainable than Cathay, and in all likelihood pleasanter; meanwhile rolling along in Mrs. Blazer's chariot, which was like a hugh bath-tub on wheels.

Morning at Newport is a disorganized period, in which the general gathering at the Casino about midday is the most definite incident. Strangers wander about uneasily; now and then a dashing equipage speeds along Bellevue Avenue, or a hired victoria creeps languidly through that thoroughfare. The coachmen and footmen attached to the dashing equipages glide rigidly onward in their appointed places; the grooms jump up or down, open doors, and fold their arms, with all the precision of trained monkeys; their yellow-topped boots, many-buttoned liveries and "bug"-adorned hats increasing the likeness. There are also a good many young men on the street who bear a close resemblance to these hired attendants: their dress, though different, is just as artificial, and they are just as much bound to conduct themselves according to an arbitrary fashion. It is the height of luxury for human beings who have the requisite means to distort other human beings who take care of their horses and carriages, — on the same principle that once made it the fashion at European courts to keep dwarfs, who had been specially stunted and twisted to meet the demand. The young men of the avenue, finding no one else to distort them, have to do it for themselves. They are debarred from becoming lackeys, but they enjoy all the appearance of being employed on salaries to make themselves absurd.

There they go, trotting about in their small, tight-waisted cutaways, or in long-tailed Incroyable coats, that give them a playful likeness to moths of an exaggerated size. Their shoulders are held awkwardly forward; they lift their tight little legs and stamp their small, uncomfortable shoes down on the pavement with studied over-earnestness, producing a startling imitation of persons who really have a purpose in going somewhere. They cling each one to a small cane, with a certain desperate tenacity that makes you suspect it is a sort of perch, to which they have grown accustomed in the cage where they served their apprenticeship. But what are we talking about? Are not these little creatures men? Most assuredly they wear that painful look of experience so carefully assumed by an order of animals nearly approaching man; and we must give them the benefit of the doubt.

During the forenoon large covered wagons, with romantic names sprawled along their sides, — the Amarintha, the Margarita, the Madeline, — had proudly caracoled through the streets, carrying a motley freight of people still ignorant and innocent enough to ride down to Easton's Beach for a surge-bath; but now these lordly vehicles, their brief hour of triumph having passed, withdrew into obscurity, giving way to the veritable curule aristocracy. The little creatures, also, with their tight legs and tiny sticks and slender coat-tails, made haste either to get places in the driving throng, or to ensconce themselves on the reading-room veranda or in the Casino Club windows, where they could view the procession with placid superiority.

Gradually the soft crushing of wheels and the tapping sound of delicately stepping horses, which had at first been intermittent, merged into a continuous, subdued whir: the main part of Bellevue Avenue and broad, old-time Kay Street, with its sober mansions and retired-looking cottages, were filled by an unbroken stream of moving carriages. The sunlight glinted on the polished harness metal and abundant varnish of tilburys, dog-carts, landaus, gigs; and even basket-wagons were to be seen here and there, swimming along in the black, glittering tide. Quisbrough and Judge Malachi Hixon, sitting democratically on the long piazza of the Ocean House, — the Judge with his hat and chair both tipped comfortably back and his feet entangled in the railing, — observed the procession. Mary Deering was out in her village-cart, driving Atlee, who surveyed the scene with such perfection of acquired gravity that his very eye-glass seemed to cast a shadow over every thing. Soon afterwards they saw Congressman Overblow jolting along on the back seat of a T-cart, while his enormous spouse occupied a place in front beside the hook-nosed gentleman who was directing the horse. Overblow smoked a very large cigar and appeared to think that he was in the height of the style. On went the cavalcade. Vivian Ware had chosen to make herself conspicuous by appearing on horseback, attended by Count Fitz-Stuart; and Justin Craig, who was strolling along the sidewalk in his loose, dowdy apparel, on the lookout for her, did not even receive a nod from the fair face under the tall hat. Jospehine Hobart flashed by in company with a young man who appeared to be greatly devoted to her, but left on the minds of spectators, as he skimmed the edge of the crowd, only the impression of a long red mustache flying through the air. There was no occasion for remark in her being with him, for everybody knew him as Roland De Peyster, whose ambition it was to secure for his tilbury more pretty girls in the season than should fall to the lot of any other young bachelor; but he had no intention of lavishing his great fortune on any single damsel. "I can't marry, you know," he would sometimes say. "It would turn the head of the best girl I could pick; so I try to preserve them in all their perfection as they are."

There were many lovely women in the procession, and many bows and smiles were exchanged; but there were likewise hidden animosities and heart-burnings lurking under the gay costumes and flowers of the women and the reticent coats of the men. Sundry youths of the most eligible pattern had failed to secure desirable partners for the course, and drove in solitary grandeur. Raish Porter was also alone, but he looked the personification of contentment; his penetrating eyes took in every thing, but his bearded, hearty face gave him the air of an indulgent master of the ceremonies, a person who watched the machinery and helped to keep it going for the benefit of others. Quisbrough pointed out to Judge Hixon Mrs. Ballard Mole, a devoted churchwoman, who was airing the Bishop of Alaska in a heavy barouche, presided over by two servants in deep black, with wrinkled black gloves and equally wrinkled visages, doleful as those of hired mourners. But just as he had done so, the inane tooting of a horn was heard; and the four-in-hand of Colonel Clancy lumbered into view, bearing on its high back a large party who appeared to have fled to that eminence in order to escape some threatened inundation. They were closely pursued by the Baron de Huyneck, the Austrian ambassador; and a stout individual not far behind, who might have been taken for a prosperous old-clothes dealer from Chatham Street, turned out to be Rustuffi Bey, representative of the Sublime Porte. It was natural enough that Mrs. Farley Blazer should happen to pass at about the same time with the other diplomatists; but it may be be imagined how insignificant Oliphant must have felt in such a train. Still, he was permitted something of that awful joy which small boys on the outside of a circus experience in peeping under some lifted fold of the tent. He knew he had not paid his share for the performance, but he was getting the benefit of it, all the same. Millions of dollars, and various things besides, had been contributed by the others. Trade, law, religion, social ambition, politics, honor, — possibly dishonor, — thrift and idleness, were all in that stream; and those who stood for such diverse interests had probably scrificed a good deal in order to join the rout. What power was it, mightier than horses' legs, that drew them on, and whither were they drifting?. That was what the atom Oliphant inwardly inquired; and in the thickest part of the press he was suddenly reminded of an engraving after Boulanger, which he had noticed in the house of a friend. It depicted the Appian Way crowded with chariots and litters, fleet Nubian slaves and fashionable idlers and beautiful women, at the time of Rome's greatest luxury, before the fall. No doubt the architecture and the costumes were very different, but there was an element of sameness in the pictured scene and this real one: here, too, were the reigning beauties and the handsome, selfish young men and the slaves — the last from Britannia and Hibernia, instead of Nubia, and wearing more than the simple waist-cloth that satisfied Rome. And might not Overblow, with his big cigar, take the place of Boulanger's bull-necked senator? Oliphant laughed at the burlesque truth in his fancy. What he saw before him, after all, was only a parody upon the Roman scene; a modern comic opera, mounted at great expense and ridiculing the old notion that luxury implies decadence.

"What are you laughing at?" Mrs. Blazer asked, coming out of a brief pre-occupation. "Oh, I see," she added, immediately: "you recognize your friends."

In fact, as she put her question, Oliphant was taking off his hat to Octavia, who, enthroned upon a high seat with Thorburn, swept by them in the neighboring line of carriages, going the other way. Her face was radiant, and she gave him an enchanting smile and bow. Then he saw her no more.

"No," said Oliphant, becoming almost grave; "I was laughing at an ancient joke — a joke at least two thousand years old."

"Ah," said the matron, "that was before my time. What can it be?"

"The joke of thinking society is serious."

"I wish I could see the fun in that," Mrs. Blazer observed.

"So do I," returned Oliphant; "for if you did you might be happier." And the smile came back to his lips.

We need not be deceived by his tone. At that instant he was by no means in a jocose mood; and, in fact, if he and Octavia had leaned from their carriages as they passed, and had wounded each other with rapiers, the encounter could not have been more startling than it proved for both of them.

He was amazed to see her abroad at all; especially to see her so apparently contented. Although he had not wanted her to suffer, it shocked him that she should so easily surmount the pain she must have felt; and possibly he was thwarted in some unconscious scheme of acting as a consoler. Add to this that her being with Thorburn, and the possibility that the heavily gilded youth might be making headway in his suit for her hand, quickened the sentiment already smouldering in Oliphant's breast. From the ashes in his heart an impassioned envy, a new hope, broke like a spurt of flame.

Octavia, in turn, was horrified that he should openly parade in Mrs. Blazer's company. What did all his protestations of strict concealment amount to, weighed against his presence there with the woman who had first hinted to her the gossip concerning Gifford's former attachment to Miss Davenant? Octavia believed strongly in feminine intuitions, particularly when she was constructing an opinion of her own. She saw it all now; she was positive that Oliphant had weakly allowed Mrs. Blazer to extract the whole history from him. The bitterness of this thought, stinging her mind even as she bowed to him, had a peculiar result: it caused her to throw additional sweetness into her smile.

"Who is that Oliphant, any way?" inquired the blonde young Crœsus at her side, as they drove along. "Seems to me, if any man could reasonably claim the right to be jealous about you, there would be some cause for alarm, just now. I think Mr. Oliphant will be falling in love with you in about two twos from the present moment — or say in one shake of a ram's tail."

"Perry," said Octavia, "if you expect to talk with me, you really must correct your slang. But what makes you think that about Mr. Oliphant?"

"Oh, the way he looked at you. How can I tell what makes me think it, anyhow? Let's talk about Josephine. You say that her father really insists on her going back to Jamestown. How soon?"

"In a few days, at the outside. He's inexorable."

The young man looked meditative. "Well, what am I to do?" he began, after a pause. "I hardly dare to venture on speaking to her so soon. Would you advise me to?"

"My friend," said Octavia, "is any one ever old enough to advise in such matters? Besides, you know" — here the young widow slightly tossed back her head and laughed aloud, so that the short white veil that scarcely touched her lips was shaken by the merriment — "she's supposed to be engaged to Lord Hawkstane!"

People in the neighboring carriages, though they could not distinguish what she said, heard her laugh ring out, and turned to look at the white throat, swelling like a song-bird's, at the trim figure, the dainty costume, the roses blooming in her corsage.

"The devil!" exclaimed Thorburn. "I beg pardon; but that's hardly slang, because — because the devil is eminently the proper thing nowadays. Is it positively true, though, about Josephine and Hawkstane?"

I regret to say that the clatter of harness and hoofs and the crunching of wheels made Octavia's reply inaudible.

By this time Mrs. Blazer and Oliphant were far away in the opposite direction, and were entering upon the road that leads to Castle Hill; but they had continued to converse about the two people we have just been listening to.

"You knew Mrs. Gifford before, I believe," remarked Mrs. Blazer.

"Before when? No; I never saw her until I came to Newport."

"But Mr. Gifford was acquainted with your wife, I hear."

"What!" cried Oliphant. "You have found it out, too? I wonder if there is anybody left in Newport who hasn't been told of that interesting circumstance."

"I imagine it is known to very few," said Mrs.

Blazer quietly, with a rather wicked glimmer in her weary eyes, peering out from the dull, white face.

"Seriously, then," he resumed, "will you tell me from whom you learned it?"

Mrs. Blazer attempted pleasantry. "You were just saying, Mr. Oliphant, that it's foolish to take society *au sérieux.*"

"Well, I suppose it is. But I'm not a society man; and this is not a public matter, you assure me, though it had begun to seem like one when you mentioned it."

"Don't you remember," she resumed, "that I told you how Mr. Sweetser knew all about you?"

"Ah, it was from him, was it? But he couldn't have known of the"— Oliphant was on the point of saying "the letter." He made a new approach. "One question occurs to me: have you spoken of this to Mrs. Gifford, at all?"

"Mrs. Gifford? Why, that would be the most natural thing in the world, wouldn't it? Yes, I think I did say something." How artlessly Mrs. Blazer answered!

"I'm exceedingly sorry. I don't think you should have done it," said he, biting his lip.

"If I had had any idea it could annoy you," the lady replied, benignly, "of course I wouldn't have uttered a word."

"Do you consider it strange that I should be annoyed? Perhaps it isn't necessary for me to go into the reasons why I am. But I really shall have to ask you how much you may have said to Mrs. Gifford."

"What a singular question! You seem to be disturbed, Mr. Oliphant. Well, I'll tell you: I hardly said more to Mrs. Gifford than I have to you."

"Your answer is as strange as my question," said Oliphant. He was at a loss to guess how Octavia had been apprised that there was a letter, if it had not been through Mrs. Blazer. Then, reverting to the possibility that Raish had found out something, "Did your information," he inquired, "come only from Mr. Sweetser?"

"From whom else should you imagine?" Mrs. Blazer retorted. "Of course he was my informant."

"The only one?" Oliphant fixed his eyes upon her.

His companion shifted the position of her parasol by a point or two, and bowed in her grand manner to the Baron de Huyneck, who had made a turn and was coming back. "Dear me," she replied, languidly, "I know very little about this affair. I only mentioned it because it happened to come into my head. I thought it might make conversation."

"And so it did," Oliphant answered. "I have been put in a disagreeable position of late, by this very thing, because some one has spoken of what I had supposed was to be guarded sacredly. You will greatly oblige me if you will give me a direct reply."

"I'm sorry to refuse," said Mrs. Blazer, "but I cannot see why I should be mixed up with it, any way."

Oliphant's suspicion was strengthened by her behavior. The conviction that it was Mrs. Blazer who had carried every thing to Octavia, and the belief that she had purposely inveigled him into public companionship with her, mortified and enraged him. He laid his hand on the lever of the carriage door.

"What are you going to do?" demanded the owner of the carriage, in alarm.

"I'm going to take my leave, and walk back," said he.

"Oh, don't! don't!" she exclaimed. "You will kill yourself! Wait a moment. Andreas," she called to the coachman, "stop here: we are going to turn."

"Thanks," said Oliphant. "You mustn't inconvenience yourself; I prefer to get down." He already had the door open, and, as Andreas reined in the horses, he placed his foot on the step. "You have nothing more to tell me?" he queried, looking up at her with hostile fixity.

"Nothing," declared Mrs. Blazer, and firmly contracted those uneasy lips of hers. At this, Oliphant sprang to the ground.

"Drive on, Andreas," Mrs. Blazer commanded; and, while Oliphant lifted his hat with grim ceremony, the impressive bath-tub on wheels started forward again, its occupant settling herself to face the sea-breeze alone.

He strode along the highway in a fierce temper. All the soft serenity of the afternoon did not avail to soothe him; and when he regained the sidewalk of Bellevue Avenue, where the well-bred rumble and clatter of the polished turn-outs were still going on, the sight of that respectable pageant redoubled his disgust. "What a fool I am," he muttered, "to care about all this! Why do I bother myself about Mrs. Gifford, and why can't I just look on and amuse myself with the mock-Roman Newport holiday? Or else, why don't I get away from here at once, and leave the whole thing behind me?" But something told him he could not go; it was too late; he had been trapped, fascinated, he hardly knew how. The rest of the world looked strangely empty, as he imagined himself going out into it again. Desolate though it had been to him before, he had not conceived until this instant that it could seem quite so vacant.

All at once Octavia appeared before him a second time, not as a vision, but as a delightful reality. Thorburn had decided to take the Ocean drive, and they had changed their direction accordingly. Away they flew, and Oliphant had only time enough for a glimpse of her. He thought her absorbed in conversation with Perry; too much so, indeed. He did not know that they were still talking more or less directly about Josephine Hobart; nor was he aware that they had both observed him and exchanged comments at his re-appearance on foot, so soon after they had seen him with Mrs. Blazer.

"I swear!" observed Perry. "Came back on purpose to see *you*."

"Nonsense," said Octavia. "He has forgotten something he had to do; or perhaps Mrs. Blazer only took him up by chance, for a little way."

Her heart fluttered, though she saw no reason for its doing so; and, bending her head as if to keep the wind off her face, she avoided meeting Oliphant's gaze. As for him, he proceeded on his way still more disconsolately; and when he came opposite the Casino entrance, the desire to get out of sight and be quiet moved him to pass into the deserted enclosure.

Another unhappy lover had gone in there, just a little before — in fact, our friend Justin Craig; and the two met, not many paces from the Clock-Tower. Oliphant observed that the young musician looked peculiarly excited, as he came forward. "See here, what I have found!" cried Justin, stretching forth his hand.

As Oliphant had passed the ticket-taker's window, he had caught sight of a white paper on the wall, announcing the loss of a lady's diamond pin, for the recovery of which a large reward was offered. What Justin now disclosed in his artistic palm was apparently the very jewel described.

"You've found it, eh?" said the widower. "Ah, you rascal, to take advantage of seeing the notice before I did! That was what brought you in, I suppose — hunting for this thing."

Justin's face grew pink. "I didn't see any notice at all," he said, rather gruffly. "Where?"

Oliphant pointed towards the small spot of paper. "At any rate, my boy," said he, "you're five hundred dollars better off than you were before you stepped in here: that's the reward. And I'm glad of it. But how did you happen upon the discovery?"

"Well, the fact is, I felt blue, I — I don't care to explain why; and so I got reckless and spent half a dollar to come in here — half a dollar is a good deal to me, you know. I was mooning around, looking at the grass and the flowers, and trying to be unconscious of those swell waiters over in the café windows: there were two of them laughing at my clothes, I know they were." Justin's manner here became quite ferocious, and he glared disdainfully at the restaurant side of the building. "There's one comfort," he said: "the wretches are forced to wear dress-coats in the daytime; so they're as much out of fashion as I am. Well, I was looking into that flower-bed close by the balcony, when I saw a twinkle and flash in the dark earth. I thought it was a dewdrop, at first; it threw out that same sort of gleam. Do you know how beautiful the dew is, Mr. Oliphant? I often walk out very early in the morning to see it on the fields; it is so glorious. You'd think gems had been scattered there over night — rubies and emeralds and topazes and beryls and the rest of 'em; but there's no pride or envy connected with them. Ah, it's one of my greatest pleasures!"

"But the diamonds," Oliphant reminded him, quietly amazed at his young friend's indifference. "You're forgetting about those."

Justin looked down at the shining cluster in his hand. "Oh," he said, smiling, "I thought I had explained. Of course there couldn't be any dew at this time of day: it turned out to be these diamonds, almost buried in the mould. They probably slipped from some lady's dress, as she was standing on the balcony above. Now, there's a nice idea, to think how horribly she must feel about it, and how happy she'll be when she gets them back!"

Oliphant laughed, his amazement turning to pleasure. "Upon my word," he declared, "I believe if it weren't for that idea, you'd be sorry they were diamonds, instead of dewdrops. You don't seem to think any thing about the reward."

"The reward! That's true: I suppose it's fair to take it, if it's worth the sum to her to get them back."

"Of course it's worth that much and more. The stones must have cost four or five thousand, Justin; and five hundred" —

"Did you mean that?" Justin broke in, grasping his arm. "I thought you were joking. Five hundred dollars in a lump! Why, it's a fortune to me! I can do all sorts of things; I can go to Germany and study." He held his breath for an instant. "But then I should have to leave" — He stopped.

"Of course you'd have to 'leave,' if you were going. Leave what?"

"Home," said Justin shyly. "Something else, too — a great deal more to me than that."

"Oh, I see," said his companion. "I wonder who the lady is."

"That I sha'n't tell you," Craig retorted, presenting a warlike front. He saw his mistake, however, instantly.

"I meant the lady who lost the jewel," Oliphant told him; and they joined in a laugh of good understanding.

"I hardly like this idea, though," Craig resumed, "of accepting money for restoring what isn't mine. It seems to put one in a false position."

"Not in your case," argued his friend. "I think it would be wrong for you to refuse. You must consider the money as a tax levied by Providence for the encouragement of art."

They proceeded in a very cheerful humor to the superintendent's office; for the incident of the finding had temporarily driven off Oliphant's agitations concerning Octavia, and had almost made Craig forget the misery of having been met by Vivian Ware without recognition.

"I see," he began, to the clerk, "that a diamond brooch has been lost. Can you tell me the name of the owner?"

The clerk looked up at him with experienced insolence. "See here, young man," said he, "do you think I'm fresh?"

"No," said Craig. "I should think you were particularly faded. Does that suit you any better?"

The official youth was surprised at such audacity in a mere citizen, badly dressed. He looked closer at the two gentlemen, and saw that Oliphant's costume and appearance were deserving of respect. "I thought you were a newspaper chap," he remarked somewhat apologetically to Craig, "picking up items. Do you know any thing about that brooch?"

"I should like to know something about it, because I have found one here."

"You have, hey?" returned the clerk, becoming briskly companionable. "That's all right, then. You're in for the reward, I guess. Well, the lady that lost it is Mrs. Chauncey Ware. Know her?"

A change came over Craig's manner. He stiffened, glanced quickly at Oliphant, and then back at the clerk. "There is the brooch I found," he said, holding it up for the man's inspection. "I shall not take any reward."

The clerk suppressed a whistle of astonishment, and put his hand forward to receive the diamonds.

"Just wait a minute," interposed Oliphant. "This is a matter for one of the governors. You needn't deliver the pin here, Craig. Besides," he continued in a lower tone, "I protest against your declining the reward."

Craig was pale and rather agitated. "Do you know," he returned, with a cold gleam in his eyes, "who Mrs. Ware is? She is the mother of Vivian Ware; and if I had to starve first, I would never accept a dollar from her, under any circumstances."

They had stepped away a little, so that the clerk behind the desk should not hear. ". Take a little time, my boy; think," said Oliphant, with a hand on his shoulder. "You will find my name down," he added, to the clerk, "as a subscriber; and I will be responsible for the delivery of this brooch. Or you can send for one of the governors, and we will wait up-stairs. Here's my card."

"All *right*, sir," said the companionable clerk.

"No, we won't wait at all!" thundered Craig, vehemently. "I've found the brooch, and I'll have nothing more to do with it. Mr. Oliphant, you ought to understand me!" And as he spoke, he brought to bear upon his friend the ardor and the softness of his fine eyes, in which could be read a confession of his love for Vivian, and all the piteous struggle of his wounded pride and social disadvantage. "There!" he wound up; "take the pin, and manage it as you prefer. I don't wish my name mentioned; and I'm going."

Oliphant looked at him reproachfully, but Craig thrust the precious object into his hands and stalked quickly away, making for the street. "At least, Craig — look here!" called his friend. "I want you to dine with me at seven, here in the Casino. Will you come?"

Craig halted. "In these clothes?" he inquired sarcastically.

"In any thing — a bathing-suit, if you like."

Justin's magnificence broke down at this. "I'll be with you," he said, emitting a short, pleased laugh. But, having done that much, he continued on his way, and disappeared.

Oliphant waited until he could see the superintendent and assure him of the safety of the brooch; and after that he hastened to the house of Mrs. Chauncey Ware. He found her engaged, but Stillman, whom he had met at Raish's lunch, received him. Stillman Ware, who was about twenty-eight, looked forty years old: he had a wrinkled brow and black hair which was alarmingly scant on the crown of his head; and he wore mild, unobtrusive little shiny shoes. There was a general air about him as if he had been finished in patent leather; he also bore his premature aging with the imperturbableness of a trained gentleman; indeed, with something of pleasantry, as if conscious that he had got a good deal of fun out of life, even though he had drawn heavily on his principal to pay for it. He accepted the news of Justin's refusal to take the reward with a kind of sweet annoyance. He was very gentle, but very much provoked.

"Mr. Craig," he said, "may be an excellent person, but I don't see why he should assume the tone of a man of wealth. I am told he is quite straitened as to his means. And it is scarcely fair for him to insist on placing us under an obligation which we can't repay."

"Will you dine with me this evening, and meet him?" Oliphant asked. "I think you would like him, and you might talk it over."

"Thanks; I am engaged for dinner. However, my mother or I will perhaps see him to-morrow. There is a particular reason why we cannot accept a favor of this kind at his hands. It's all wrong. He *must* allow us to recompense him."

"And the particular reason?" Oliphant began. "I suppose I ought not to inquire what it is."

"I would rather not say," answered Ware. "Perhaps you have some inkling of it already."

This was the gist of their interview, which soon came to an end. In the evening, Justin professed annoyance that Oliphant should have disclosed his name as that of the finder; but this wore off, and the result of their session at dinner was a long walk together under the starlight, and a talk in which Oliphant made his way to Justin's confidence.

"I stand alone in the world, Craig," he said to him, "and if you will make a friend of me I shall be in your debt for giving me a new interest. With me the best of life is over, but perhaps I can help your cause with Vivian; and if you succeed in music through any passing assistance I may lend, don't you see how great my pleasure would be in that success?"

They were pausing, about to part, by the mysterious Old Mill, or Norseman's Tower, in Touro Park. The carriages, coaches, and phaetons which had filed past it so numerously a few hours before had now utterly disappeared; there was no more tramping of horses; not a trace of the pageant remained. A village quiet, in fact, reigned over Newport, broken only at the moment by the meagre, sharp, and grating notes of a chorus of tree-toads. Electric lights, however, suspended on high poles, threw a weird illumination down upon the dew-damp street, or across and under the muffling foliage of the trees, in wide splashes and long, jagged streaks, as if the radiance were a liquid that had undergone icy crystallization. In this cold light the face of Justin shone for an instant with responsive gratitude: he seemed to accept the position of a younger brother towards his companion.

"Your sympathy and fellowship are help enough," he said, pressing Oliphant's hand.

Then the lighted face turned and passed away down the dark street, and Oliphant's eyes rested on the dim tower which confronted him like a ghost of gray stone, looking as if it had a warning to utter. But what of that? Faces come and go around the old tower, or vanish forever from its presence, while it remains unaltered, a perpetual enigma of the past. And are not the faces enigmas, just as much? And has not love its gray ruins, that loom up in the night and seem on the point of warning us? But no one would heed the warning, even if it ever came to speech.

VII.

LORD HAWKSTANE'S JUST PRIDE.

MRS. CHAUNCEY WARE was a woman of high social position in Boston; she had abundant wealth; she was attended by a train of obsequious ancestors and subservient living personages. Her face was colorless except for a lingering brown tinge, and was quilted all over with fine lines that seemed to have been arranged by a pattern; so that you might have fancied for a moment that it was itself an heirloom, some kind of a sampler or old piece of stitching, carefully preserved until it had grown rather dingy. Further reflection would convince you that the surface was human, after all, but that peculiar influences slowly working upon it had imparted a strangeness and imperviousness that made it appear unreal.

It was a comfortable, satisfied countenance, as well it might be, for the prevailing superstition in the three-hilled city attributed to its possessor an amount of visiting-list and old-family wisdom never surpassed by any other conservator of society. Mrs. Ware always exhibited two cylindrical puffs of grayish hair on her temples; minute sibylline scrolls, one might say. Somehow, in those two puffs, which were like insignia of her high office, she appeared to have coiled up the experience of a life-time; and Raish Porter had once alluded to them as the steel-gray mainsprings of her existence.

It may easily be imagined how such a person, knowing in a distant and austere way that Craig cherished a preposterous sentiment for her daughter, must have felt with regard to his obstinacy about the reward. "I entirely agree with Stillman," she said, the next morning, at breakfast. "The young man should be made to take it."

She regarded her son with instructive gravity, as if it were he whom she desired to convince, instead of her daughter. The gently polished Stillman, who had staid out late the night before, gambling heavily, seemed to have become indifferent on the subject.

"'Made to take it,' mamma?" said Vivian. "One would almost suppose he had committed an offence by finding your pin and sending it to you. *I* think he has a right to refuse, if he wants to — the right that any gentleman would have."

"Is he any? If so, how many?" her brother asked, trying to relieve the tedium of the discussion.

"Stillman, I fear for your mind," said Vivian. "Don't you think it is tottering just a little bit?" She contemplated him with a pretty, unconcerned scorn, then devoted herself wholly for the moment to a rye-and-Indian roll.

"I shall believe it is tottering, my excellent sister," he replied, "when I find myself convinced by you."

His savageness did not humiliate her, but she tried

a pathetic appeal, quite as if she had actually been humiliated. "You wouldn't like to take money yourself, in that way, would you?" she demanded, bending earnestly forward, and giving him a look for which Craig would have walked fifty miles.

"Wouldn't I?" returned the patent-leather cynic, unmoved. "Just let mother try offering it to me. I dropped twice that sum at roulette, last night."

"Stillman," said Mrs. Ware, in a tone of conventional grief, "I wish you wouldn't allude to those things."

He smiled, complacently. "You know, mother, I never make any secret of my amusements. It is only serious things that one cares to conceal."

"That is quite epigrammatic," his sister observed, thinking it best to flatter him. "But, mamma, why not just thank Mr. Craig, and let the whole thing go?"

"Or," suggested Stillman, attempting an extreme of sarcasm, "you might invite him to your party to-night."

"Not a bad idea, either," Vivian commented.

"What absurdity!" exclaimed her mother.

"Oh, I've no doubt Vivian is longing to have him here. She is greatly interested in him, beyond a question."

"So is Mrs. Gifford," Vivian retorted. "And why shouldn't I be? It was she who first made me acquainted with him; don't you remember?"

"I wish she had been in Guinea!" affirmed Mrs. Ware, in a large geographical spirit. "A strange freak of hers, that was; and your allowing him to call here, Vivian, was still stranger. But then, I long ago learned that I needn't expect you to be judicious. You will never outgrow your girlhood, my child."

Vivian, who had at that instant conveyed a dainty morsel to her lips, was seized with something like a choking fit. When this threat had been averted, she was seen to be laughing. "I assure you, mamma," she cried, "you almost made me swallow my fork; and then what would you have done? Outgrow my girlhood? I hope I shall not. I mean always to be young. Dear me, this is too funny!" Mrs. Ware's wisdom-curls appeared to wind themselves tighter than ever, in view of a levity so abandoned; but Vivian, still afflicted with laughter, rose from her place and turned — her gayly colored baptiste gown making a graceful sweep — to the bird-cage in the window behind her. "Poor little canary," she murmured, "you haven't had your morning bath and your fresh chickweed, have you? And all this time we are talking about trivial matters." Here she cast a swift glance at her mother again, and remarked tersely, "As if I were in any way responsible for Mr. Craig! You may count me out."

"Stillman, will you go down to see him?" Mrs. Ware asked, in a confidential tone, ignoring Vivian.

"I'm sorry, mother, but I have so much to do about our affair this evening, you know."

"Then *I* shall go," she announced. "It is proper that the young man should be thanked, at any rate, if he won't accept more."

Go she did, accordingly. Justin was summoned

from an abstruse piece of counterpoint on which he was laboring, to confront the undecipherable face and the gray puffs, which had emerged from the Ware chariot just drawn up at his humble boarding-house door; and at first his visitor endeavored to give their meeting a briefly business-like turn. "I am very much obliged to you," she said, "for recovering an ornament that I value especially for its associations, and I have come in person to hand you the sum we had named as the reward, because I wanted to have the opportunity of thanking you for your service."

"It was no service," said Justin; "only an accident. But I appreciate your kindness in thanking me."

He spoke so simply, and in a tone so engaging, that Mrs. Ware began to be impressed. "Then, will you allow me"—she continued, hesitating slightly, as she touched the spring of the seal-skin portemonnaie she carried.

Justin was naturally somewhat dramatic in his movements. He raised one hand, with a gesture of forbidding. "No, indeed!" he responded vigorously. "I thought Mr. Oliphant had made that clear to you."

"May I ask," inquired the lady, her gloved fingers still hovering over the portemonnaie, "why you are so resolute in declining this very proper return for your favor?"

"I hardly think," he replied, calmly, "it would do any good for me to go into the reasons. I really can't see that I have done any thing to be rewarded, and you have more than paid me with your thanks."

Mrs. Chauncey Ware secretly admired his reserved and politic attitude; she felt that it lifted him up almost to her own plane. "Pardon me," she rejoined, "I do not know much of young men of your class, but I must say I wasn't prepared for this sort of feeling in one of them."

There was great danger of combustion in Justin's mind, at this instant, but he managed to prevent it. "You surprise me," he said. "If we have any such thing as distinct classes in this country, I should have thought that it was precisely with mine that you would be best acquainted."

"At all events," she returned, quite unperturbed, "it is a great satisfaction to arrive at so good an understanding." Still, Mrs. Ware had sense enough to see that she had got the worst of it, and tact enough to be conscious that there was but one way of recovering her lost ground. Besides, I believe she had a certain amount of humane sympathy left in her, which caused her to pity Justin's poverty, and to value his independence. "We will say no more about this errand on which I came," she continued, "if you prefer; but it shall be on one condition: that is, that you come to-night to a reception which I have arranged at my house."

Justin's heart leaped at the thought of such an invitation. He was perfectly aware that the sleeves of his dress-coat were very ragged inside; but no one is richer than he who, being without money, can afford to refuse it; and for the time being he felt as opulent as possible. To meet Vivian in her own house, on equal terms with all her friends, and especially the Count Fitz-Stuart! It was something not to be foregone. He did not betray his emotion; he did not spring into the air; he did not give vent to the triumphant cry that clamored within him. "I shall be very happy," he said, with exemplary self-control; but that short phrase covered a great deal of meaning.

And thus it happened that Stillman Ware's extravagant suggestion became within an hour's time sober reality, through the action of that unimpeachable authority, his mother.

"I don't know what we shall come to, if this is the sort of thing that's going to be done," he complained, when she told him of it; "which means that I do know, exactly. Vivian, whose sense of humor can't be depended on, will fall in love with that young piano-pounder, and never see the absurdity of it."

"Well, my boy, Vivian is erratic, at the best: she *will* be wild, whatever is done. Do you know what she did only yesterday? She called across the street to Colonel Clancy, who was passing, and made him go into the Casino to lunch with Roland De Peyster and herself and the Richards girls. I wonder you hadn't heard, for it came to *me* soon enough, I can tell you. But it's no use talking to her. And as for this Craig, now that he has called here he may as well be recognized. If we try to keep him out, she will think all the more of him. Besides, I had to do something to throw the obligation upon his side."

Mrs. Ware had found her son on the lawn at the back of the house, superintending the placing of some lanterns. "Very well," he said, when she finished. "I see that it's settled; but I shall have to make some changes in my plan, now: it will be necessary to put lanterns in the arbor."

"Why, what has that got to do with Craig?"

"I'll tell you," said Stillman, resignedly. "That arbor was to be left dark; I had just told the men so. It was a little experiment of mine — a trap in which I expected to catch a few song-birds. Off in that quiet corner under the trees, you see, some of the sentimental young people would be sure to make for it, if it were dark. Now that Craig is coming, though, I shall illuminate it brilliantly: no *tête-à-tête* there for *him*, with Vivian, if I can help it! But you've spoiled my fun, this time."

Oliphant was delighted with the news of Justin's invitation, but it was not the only surprise of the day, for him. At the club, about noon, he fell in with Dana Sweetser, who, chirping gayly of current incidents, spoke of the gossip concerning Lord Hawkstane's engagement.

"Amazingly lucky fellow!" he exclaimed, reviving for the occasion an ancient tremor of the voice which had once, no doubt, been capable of conveying real emotion. "On her part, however, it seems to me a mistake to accept him so early in the season. She should have waited until September. It diminishes the interest, you know: she won't be sought after as much."

Continuing, he confided the fact that he was almost heart-broken by the news; having cherished an ideal sentiment for Miss Hobart. But, in a moment or two, he began to expatiate upon the charms of Miss Loyall, the young beauty from Albany. Tiring of such discourse, Oliphant diverted him to the Alaska and British Columbia Inlet Excavation, of which Sweetser was the projector and chief advocate.

The scheme was a gigantic one: nothing less than the scooping out of a considerable territory north of the United States, so that a large inlet from the Pacific Ocean might be formed, which should modify and greatly improve the climate of this country. "A good many laborers were frozen to death at first, but it was a valuable lesson to us, as well as to them, and we have now provided against that. I have another matter in hand, though," said Dana, "for which you must interest yourself: it is the Drainage Association."

"What is the object?"

"To improve the drainage of Newport — very much needed, you know. The conditions are frightful, here. Do you appreciate, sir, that we are walking in constant peril? The whole place is threatened with an unborn pestilence — think of it! — doomed, perhaps. I'm going to agitate, and there must be an Association."

Oliphant found himself in peril from the man's enthusiasm; but Sweetser, catching sight of Lord Hawkstane, who had just entered the next room, promptly abandoned his subject and his listener, and went to offer the Englishman his congratulations. So, at least, Oliphant inferred from his effusive manner and wreathed smiles.

Hawkstane appeared embarrassed, but not displeased. Oliphant imagined that he was making some negative protestation; but Sweetser evidently thought this an excellent joke, looked very shrewd and sly, and then, with a brief gurgle of rejuvenated laughter, went off towards the writing-room. Hawkstane began to approach the place where Oliphant sat; but on the way he was stopped a second time; for Atlee, coming in from the veranda, held him with his glittering eye-glass, like an improved species of Ancient Mariner.

"Good mawning," said Atlee, in much the same tone he might have used had he been talking in his sleep.

"*How*joo do?" said Lord Hawkstane.

"Ah — ah; fine day," Atlee continued.

"Uncommonly, for this country. If you wouldn't have it so beastly hot, you know!"

Atlee assumed the helpless look which he believed to be a token of the highest breeding. He let it be understood from his manner that climate was controlled by an inferior order of forces, with which he had no connection. After an interval of sympathetic vacancy, he resumed intellectual exercise.

"Haven't had the chance to offer my congratulations befoah, melord. Allow me to do so now."

"W'y does every one congratulate me?" inquired Lord Hawkstane, politely.

"Haw, haw," said Atlee, with funereal hilarity. "Because they envy you so howibly, I dare say. Don't you think you ought to be?"

"Oh, I've no objection; not the least in the world.

I suppose I've got on better than most men." Hawkstane looked very complacent, but adjusted his shirt-collar with one finger, as if his satisfaction needed propping. "You mean Miss Hobart?" he ended.

"To be sure," Atlee answered. "You ought to be ve'y happy."

"Thanks, yes; I am very happy," said his lordship, promptly. "I don't mind it; not the least in the world."

The spurious Englishman sounded his doleful laugh once more. "I should think not," he said, carefully preserving the somnolent tone — "I should think not."

His mental resources having apparently been exhausted, he turned to the newspapers, and Hawkstane spoke to Oliphant.

"Is it true, then," Oliphant asked immediately, "that you're engaged to Miss Hobart?"

The young man colored. "Engaged?" he repeated. "What makes you think that?"

"You must excuse my bluntness," Oliphant replied. "I thought that was what you were just speaking of. It's the general opinion, I believe."

"Hang it, no! I'm not engaged," Lord Hawkstane declared with some energy, recovering his natural pallor.

Atlee dropped his newspaper, and looked over at him with a faint, embarrassed grin, at the same time reducing his facial aspect to a complete void.

"You're not!" exclaimed Oliphant. "Good heavens, why didn't you tell us that before?"

"W'y? You're the first man who has asked me any thing about it, Mr. Oliphant. And haven't I told you, directly you asked? I thought everybody knew Miss Hobart turned me off."

"But," protested Atlee, "you — you allowed me to congratulate you." (In his excitement he forgot to slur the "r.")

"My dear fellah," said Lord Hawkstane, "that was what you wanted, wasn't it? 'Pon my word, too, I think it was right enough. W'en you think how many men admire her, and how hard she is to come at, you know, I think it's a good deal to get so far as I did. 'Pon my word, now, I accept your congratulations for having been honored by a refusal. That's more than you'll ever be, Atlee. Isn't it, Mr. Oliphant?"

Whether the young aristocrat had defeated his American friends on their own ground as a sad humorist, or whether he really meant what he said, Oliphant was unable to determine; so he held his peace, and looked wise.

"I beg pahdon, you know — awfully stupid in me — pahdon," Atlee said, disjointedly.

"Hang it!" Lord Hawkstane again ejaculated. "I mean it, you know. I'm proud of it. 'Gad, it's a feather in my cap."

Meanwhile Sweetser, unable long to resist the attraction of a title, had come back from the writing-room, and had overheard the whole disclosure from the threshold. Without delay he left the club, and, in a singularly brief space of time, what he had gathered was spread through the town.

VIII.

HALF-LIGHTS.

OLIPHANT could not at once muster courage to call upon Octavia, in reply to her note; and it was with no little trepidation that he prepared to go to Mrs. Ware's party, although he had a trembling pleasure in the prospect, also. This was to be their first interview since the critical one at her house. How, then, would she treat him? Was she angry; did she suspect his judgment or sincerity, because of his appearing on the drive with Mrs. Blazer? Or would she prove lenient?

With such queries he tortured himself as diligently as if he had been a boy of twenty, and she a capricious maiden of the same age. When at last, after floating about some time in the perfumed crush of the large villa drawing-rooms, he saw her at a distance, it seemed to him that there was a shadow of forbidding, at least a lack of cordiality, in her mute greeting. But how could so lovely a form of womanhood be cruel or unkind? Oliphant would not believe it, and hastened to make his way towards her. At that instant Roland De Peyster, by the piano, was sending out a volume of baritone voice from under his waving red mustache, singing, —

> "I know not when the day shall be,
>   I know not where our eyes may meet,
>   What welcome you may give to me,
>   Or will your words be sad or sweet;
>   It may not be till years have passed,
>   Till eyes are dim, and tresses gray:
>   The world is wide, but, love, at last,
>   Our hands, our hearts, must meet some day."
>
>   (*L'istesso tempo.*)   "Some day, some day"—

and so on. It was nothing less than sardonic in De Peyster to regale the company with this sentiment, considering the number of young ladies who were ready to meet him, not "some day," but any day; yet the performance stirred Oliphant deeply. It was with a resonance of feeling in his tone that he began to speak to Octavia.

"I must apologize," he said, "for not responding immediately to your kind note. I was really planning to call to-day, but"—

"Oh, it doesn't matter, Mr. Oliphant." She appeared much more gracious, now that he was near her. "I'm afraid," she added, "I was rather hasty in sending that note. At the time, I thought we'd better meet soon; but, to tell you the truth, I changed my mind, afterwards."

A light gust of air from some open window blew in upon Oliphant's face, while she was replying, and brought a faint tang of the sea to mingle with the odor of the flowers around them. He could not tell whether it was this breath of the lonely waters, or a lurking chillness in her manner, that touched him with momentary foreboding. "I hope no oversight or any act of mine was the cause of your change," he returned.

Octavia raised her face and smiled, looking off towards the chandelier; then said, gently, "I have no fault to find."

"Because you have found one already?" he inquired. "I have discovered who told you of the matter we were. speaking about, the other day; and I must assure you, if I had known before, I never should have appeared publicly with Mrs." —

"Hsh!" said Octavia, lifting her gloved hand a little, in warning; and Oliphant discovered that Mrs. Blazer was in the act of gliding by them, on the arm of Baron Huyneck. She barely inclined her head, as she passed, and Oliphant gave the slightest possible salutation.

"Would you mind going out on the terrace?" Octavia asked. "It is stifling here." While they moved away together, she said half archly, "Have you been taking Mrs. Blazer to task for telling tales? She has put you on her black list, evidently."

"It wasn't my fault," he answered, "that we didn't quarrel outright."

Octavia made no concealment of her pleasure; though "It was wrong for you to risk *that*," she said. "Why should you quarrel on my account?"

"Why?" echoed he. "Merely because I value your regard — or the chance of it — too much to risk losing it even for something much better than Mrs. Blazer's good will."

There was a sweet, lulled look upon Octavia's face, as she listened; a look which to Oliphant, albeit he hardly dared to think he was right, seemed like one of trustful surrender. "Thank you," she murmured, not too seriously. "You are chivalrous, I see. But tell me how it was that that woman came to hear of the circumstances."

"I haven't the faintest idea," Oliphant said; and he frankly detailed the whole history of the letter, including even his half-formed suspicion of Raish. "I questioned Porter, this afternoon, without telling him what the letter was; and he didn't seem to know a thing. He faced me squarely, and said, 'It's very puzzling, and I can't help you out at all. Don't ask me to investigate, because I make it a rule never to inquire into such things; they lead to so much trouble.'"

"I can't fully trust your friend," said Octavia; "but I believe I trust you. At any rate, it is all over, now. At first I was bewildered and thought something must be done; so I was anxious to see you. Besides, I felt so *alone*, don't you know. It was a strange moment. I wanted some one to — to " —

"Advise with?" he suggested.

"Yes." Octavia's voice sank to an enticing whisper.

"I wish I could have done any thing for you," Oliphant rejoined. "I'm bitterly sorry for the whole affair, so far as my share in it goes, if it caused you pain."

Octavia gave him a glance of gratitude for his sympathy. They were standing on the terrace, now, in the subdued light from one of the drawing-room windows. "I'm sorry, too," she said, very softly, "for you. It is a very hard position that you've been placed in."

"So you acquit me, and forgive me?"

"Why shouldn't I, Mr. Oliphant? You could hardly have done otherwise than you did."

"Still," he said, "I was afraid. But if it is all right, won't you give me a little token, — one of those roses?"

A few Marshal Niel buds hung richly upon the black of her low-cut dress.

"You don't need it," Octavia lightly assured him. "I'll give you my hand; I mean I'll shake hands, if you like. But the rose would be sentimental, and sentiment, you know, is hardly for us, at our time."

She looked away from him into the night, a little sadly. Out beyond the terrace were the many-colored glow of lanterns, the thick dusk of waving tree-tops, and the forms of guests wandering about the grounds, as indistinct in the dim light of lanterns and stars as the shapes in an old tapestry. Involved in a web of radiance from the window, which was crossed by dark lines from the curtains and a spray of palm inside, she was more beautiful than ever, with her pale brown hair, her dark dress, and the gleams of white "illusion" at the bosom.

"Nonsense!" said Oliphant. "For you, at least, it's an anachronism to take that tone; and there's some hope even for me, so long as Dana Sweetser keeps up his youth. Haven't you observed him talking devotedly to Miss Loyall, this evening?"

"No, I didn't see him. But there go two young people who are better worth noticing." She nodded towards the terrace steps, where Perry Thorburn and Josephine, who had come out of the house, were moving down into the shadowy region of the lawn.

"Oh, that reminds me: how strange about the false report of Lord Hawkstane being engaged!" Octavia began to laugh, but she ceased on his asking immediately: "Is it really young Mr. Thorburn who ought to have been rumored about, instead?"

She divined his motive. With a downcast face, as if making confession on her own behalf, she answered: "Mr. Thorburn is greatly interested in Josephine. But you're not to mention it; he confides in me."

It was indeed a confession, for it explained every thing to Oliphant; it showed him that Perry's attentions to Octavia were simply in the interest of his attachment for Josephine, and it set him free to think of Octavia as his fancy, in its most sanguine mood, might urge. Did she know the full force of this admission? Did she guess what unpremeditated scheme and infatuated longing it aroused in Oliphant? He could not tell, but was content to yield himself to the fascination of that which he imagined might be possible. And so he paced around, and smiled and chatted and sighed, and allowed various expressions to master his countenance, like other men who were present that evening; never suspecting that the women with whom he conversed — among them this charming lady, who had suddenly become for him the one apart from all the rest — were so many packages of emotional dynamite, artfully encased in silk, and set by invisible clock-work of the heart to explode at a given time.

Justin, meanwhile, had been fairly well received. He brought for Vivian a bunch of grasses and flower-de-luce and late June roses, gathered specially for her, which was so unlike every thing else in the rooms that it gained a distinction and charm of its own; and she took it with a candid little burst of thanks and friendliness. Mrs. Ware met him with haughty benevolence, and Stillman yielded him a reluctant courtesy. All had gone well, yet Justin was not happy; for Count Fitz-Stuart had appropriated Vivian, and her younger lover grudged the moments which she was now squandering on that fragment of misdirected royalty in the lamp-lit walk.

"Have you succeeded in entertaining yourself, count?" Vivian asked, as they strolled together.

"No, mademoiselle. I find your assembly charming, but when not until now have I had two words with you, sall you expect me to be content?"

"Why not? There are surely a great many pleasant people for you to talk to here. Still, no; I should think you would be tired of this country."

"Not at all. How often, mademoiselle, must I persuade you? I find Newport very agreeable — quite at the manner of Europe; *seulement un peu plus simple, savez-vous?* more — more *rustique.*"

"Then really, count, are you not longing to return home?"

"*Mais* — why do you think?"

"Because, as you're the last of your family, you must be lonesome without relatives, and I should imagine you would feel it all the more among strangers."

"No, not that," said Fitz-Stuart, with gravity. "Even if I were prince, I think I would become republican, to be near where you are."

"It would be a great pity, though," said Vivian. "We shouldn't care half as much about you, then. We Americans just adore the nobility. I'm sure *I* do. There!"

The count displayed his peachy little smile. "To be adored is ravishing," he remarked, complacently.

"Ah, but I don't say," laughed Vivian, impelled by a sense that she was engaged in one of those international encounters which have assumed such importance of late, — "I don't say that I adore *you*, you know. It's only the nobility as an institution, a class. I adore them all at once, don't you see?"

"That is too many," he said, methodically. "I prefer if you like only me."

"Oh, yes, I know. You have told me so several times."

"Ah, Mademoiselle Ware," Fitz-Stuart began with pathos, "why can you not reconsider?" As they were constantly passing other pairs, he thought it prudent to speak in French. "I have your brother's consent; I still place myself at your feet — my title, my illustrious race, every thing but fortune."

Vivian assumed alarm, and stopped him. "Don't, *don't* speak French!" she exclaimed. "Every one here knows French. Talk in English, and they will never understand you."

"Ah, these young girls of America!" murmured the count, shrugging his shoulders. "You tell me this, when my race should be upon the English throne?"

"They *would* have been there, too," Vivian hastened to say, "if James the Third, or somebody, hadn't refused to give up Catholicism, and preferred the French language. He was an ancestor of yours, wasn't he?"

The count put on the most regal manner at his disposal. "Yes, my friend," was his reply. "His majesty would not surrender his belief of religion. Does it not prove he was a good man?"

"I'm not certain," she returned. "It proves that he *thought* he was good. Perhaps you think you're good, too, Monsieur le Comte; but I never will marry a Catholic."

"Mademoiselle," said he impressively, "what my ancestor has refused to abandon for the sake of a kingdom, I will sacrifice if I can win your hand."

The speech was so magnificent that Vivian blushed with pride in spite of herself; but she answered gayly, "You'd better not forsake your religion to-night. Wait just a few days. I am sure I can't agree to what you ask — certainly not now. But I'll tell you what I *will* do. If I can't consent to marry, I'll promise to ride with you to the polo-match to-morrow, as you proposed this morning."

Fitz-Stuart contemplated her mournfully. "Mees Ware," he said, "you have no sentiment. But I submit myself."

As they regained the terrace, Vivian paused, and with a deep breath, looking up to the sky, she murmured, "How beautiful the stars are to-night!"

Again the count regarded her, thoughtfully, as if he could not make out what was passing in her mind. At length he said wearily, himself glancing at the firmament, "Yes, yes; the stars. But *they are so old!*"

"Monsieur le Comte," said Vivian, soberly, "*you* have no sentiment!"

It was after this that Justin had his chance for a short interview with her. Stillman, patrolling the house and the illuminated portion of the grounds, was especially pleased with the lighted arbor, which was to prevent any conference between his sister and Craig; but while he was sauntering along by it, with his uncovered bald head showing in the radiance like a very large pink wafer, Vivian innocently wandered away with Craig into the dark and deserted space lying on the other side of the house, along the seafront.

"It's pleasanter here," she said, "I want to get rid of that babble of voices for a little while, and listen to the waves instead."

"I don't care so much for the waves," Justin answered, significantly; "but one voice is better than many. The last time I saw you, I began to think I shouldn't hear much more of it."

"When? And what do you mean?"

"Why, yesterday, on the avenue. You rode by without noticing my existence."

"You foolish boy! You can't expect that I should

be recognizing people *all* the time. If I were, I shouldn't be able to do any thing else."

Vivian treated him to a glance of pretty disdain, which was lost in the darkness.

"There are some of the other things which I'd just as soon not have you do," said Justin.

"What, are you going to criticise me?"

"No, not you; but I might criticise the life you're leading. I don't like it. You're throwing yourself away, and it makes me very uncomfortable, besides."

"Ah, I see; there's the trouble. Men never can bear to be uncomfortable."

"You know you're not in earnest, Miss Ware, when you say that about me. But are you always going to plague me so?"

"'Always' is a long time. Perhaps we sha'n't know each other always."

"Perhaps not," said Craig, in a tone that blended with the sombreness of the night around them. "We hardly know each other now; I see you so seldom. I have to creep about in my obscure little world, and even when we meet you are surrounded by people who look down upon me. There's that count, with whom you spend so much time."

"Oh, he makes you uncomfortable, too, I suppose. But what do you imagine *he* would say, if he knew of my being out here with *you?* The count insists upon it that I ought to marry him."

"I was sure of it!" Craig exclaimed, bitterly.

"Just fancy," Vivian pursued, "how wonderful it would be to marry into a royal line — or on to the end of it, rather! We shouldn't have any court or any kingdom, but I've no doubt he would give me a real throne — if I paid for it."

"Well, with such an inducement as that, you'll probably accept him," said Justin, scornfully, but without the least conviction.

"Oh," she retorted, "you have formed a high opinion of me!"

"Vivian!" he groaned, most unexpectedly. "Don't you know? Why do I come here? Why do I wait around in places, trying to see you? Why am I miserable? Don't you know I'm in love with you?"

She held her breath for an instant. "Well," she observed, "that's a nice effect for love to have — to make you miserable!"

"Pshaw!" muttered Justin. "You understand well enough. I shouldn't be miserable at all, if you only told me that you loved me, too."

"Really?" Vivian uttered a peal of laughter, that seemed to Justin like the beginning of a new sonata. "Do you think, then, that you'd be able to endure it?"

"I don't dare to think of it," said Justin, "except when I am alone. That is, I haven't dared to, until now. But — do you love me?"

"Justin, you're not in earnest. How can I fall in love with a poor young musician, when I have counts and all sorts of rich men dancing about me? Do you think it possible?"

The poor boy was shaken with the strength of his passion, and aghast at his own temerity in declaring it so abruptly. "Oh, I don't suppose it's possible," he answered. "You know nothing of what it is to really feel: you can't be serious."

"Well, let's see if I can't," he heard her saying, without being able clearly to see her face through the night. "Why do you insist upon asking me whether I love you?"

"Because," he replied, innocently enough, "it's the only way to find out! I can't go on, without settling this question."

"Oh, that makes a difference," said Vivian, who must have had an eye like a microscope, for distinctions. "Well, then, will you listen if I tell you a great secret?" Craig said nothing, but groped for her hand and found that she allowed him to take it in his, unguarded. "Do you know," she continued, "I think — if I were to try real hard, you know, — I might like you a great deal."

"Thank Heaven!" he breathed; and the spirit of a man awoke within him. He drew her close to him.

The cool dark, the sweet odors of earth and grass, and the soothing rustle of wind and sea enveloped them with sympathy. The delicate perfume of her hair floated round him, as if she had indeed been a flower.

"How wonderful it is!" he murmured. "I can scarcely believe it; and yet it is just what I have believed, for a long time, ought to happen. But why do you think you can love me, Vivian?"

"Because you are the only true and simple man in the world," said Vivian. The reason appeared to be conclusive. "And what can you find in me?" she asked, in her turn, looking fondly up through the dusk, over his shoulder.

"It will take me all my life to explain," he said, touching his lips to her forehead. "But I must tell you," he added, "I didn't mean to speak so soon. I'm only a beginner, you know. I have nothing, and I must make my way, still."

"What does that matter?" Vivian answered. "I am well off in my own right: I shall be rich enough for both."

Both! How delicious the word sounded! But Justin felt it incumbent upon him to be austerely firm. "No," he said; "it can't be left so. I will claim nothing until I can do so fairly. Now that we are united in spirit, I won't ask you to promise: I simply trust to you. Only, see how much you can separate yourself, for me, from this gay and frivolous life in which you are placed. That's all I ask."

"Oh, you are very generous," Vivian exclaimed, moving away haughtily; "very generous, indeed! But I think I should like you all the better if you were a little — well, a little *meaner.*"

"I shall never be mean enough," he hotly rejoined, "to take an unjust advantage. If I let you engage yourself to me now, it would make you lots of trouble. Besides, think what your people would say of me!"

"Yes, that's it," Vivian was quick to say. "You care more for your pride than for me. It's very fine, this talking about love; but I've always noticed that there isn't much in it, compared with other considerations; and now I find that you're like all the rest. Yes, I was a goose; and its a humbug."

"I quite agree with you," Justin declared, becoming superbly frigid. "Women can't appreciate a manly motive. They are all self-willed and hasty, and I bitterly deceived myself in thinking you were different."

"Very well," she continued; "you wish me to be free, and I *am* free. I was going to make a great, great sacrifice for you, Mr. Craig; but now I sha'n't. I will keep my promise to the count, to ride with him to polo, to-morrow."

"Just as you please," Justin said. And they were able to return to the house in a state of polite ferocity that completely allayed Stillman's rising suspicions.

It is true, Justin played for the company, at Mrs. Ware's request, though it was not seconded by Vivian; and he had never played better, with greater fire or with profounder depth, mystery, and sentiment. "But if they only knew," he reflected, amid the ensuing applause, "how ragged my coat-linings are, and that my heart is all in tatters!"

And for a number of days afterwards it was noticed by their particular friends that both Craig and Vivian took every opportunity to point out, with convincing cynicism, the uselessness of building hopes upon the loves of men and women.

Before Oliphant went away that night, Octavia, lightly draped with a wrap that encircled her head like a hood, met him again in the hall, and, discovering that he would like to witness the polo games, invited him to lunch with Josephine and herself at High Lawn and drive to the grounds. He was exceedingly grateful for her courtesy; but the mutual relation that had sprung up between them was not yet quite clear to him. He had expected that some constraint would trammel them, after the disclosure of the letter; but, to his astonishment, there had resulted an increased freedom and intimacy, notwithstanding which he suspected that they actually stood farther apart than before. She now treated him, he was aware, with more art. "Still," he assured himself, "that is only because she feels the difficulty of putting me at my ease. Yes, yes; she's a generous woman."

IX.

POLO, AND CERTAIN POSSIBILITIES.

HALF an hour before the time for polo, the next afternoon, Perry Thorburn issued from a street near the Cliffs, driving his trap solemnly down Narragansett Avenue, accompanied by a groom with arms discreetly folded. Perry had already indued his tight-fitting riding costume, but it was entirely concealed by his long Newmarket overcoat, which allowed only the yellow-bordered boots, that projected below, to betray his errand. He held the reins, however, with peculiar gravity; he was conscious of his exalted mission; you might easily have supposed him a volunteer victim going to some heathen sacrifice, for the good of the community at large. Roland De Peyster, who was captain of the opposing side, the reds, made his entry upon the polo field from another quarter, with equal state. People in carriages, on horseback, and on foot kept assembling, until the immense enclosure within the high board fence was thickly fringed with a brilliant concourse. Bannerets fluttered from the marquees in one corner, and a band dispersed brazen melodies through the wide, warm air; there was a great array of pretty costumes, and waving ribbons, and lovely, expectant faces: the scene was festal, yet the fashionable crowd was under the spell of a subdued propriety which threw a solemn tinge over the scene. Solemnly, too, the eight players came out from the tents, and the blues rode down to the lower end of the field. Then, at a given signal, Thorburn and De Peyster charged for the centre crease, where the ball lay awaiting them.

For a few seconds nothing was heard except the dull, rapid pounding of the ponies' hoofs on the thin sward. Thud, thud, thud, they went: every one was breathless, waiting to see who should get the first stroke; but De Peyster's pony was the swiftest, and with a sharp, nervous click he sent the ball flying, before Thorburn could reach it, a good half-way towards the enemy's goal. Instantly Thorburn wheeled, and all the other players closed in. They made a queer sight, dressed in tight flannel shirts, with fantastically patterned ornament of stripes, bars, and spots, and wearing round, flat-topped caps. They appeared like so many imps starting into sudden action. Flying hither and thither, wheeling abruptly, bending forward, and skimming the ground with their long, unwieldy mallets, they scurried after the ball with the agile inconsequence of kittens, yet in deadly earnest, and never uttering a sound except a few short, sharp cries now and then, which came to the spectators as inarticulate bursts. The silence of the whole proceeding was what struck Oliphant: the punctilious, much-dressed assembly was silent, and so were the gentlemen on horseback, erratically careering about in the centre. The blues gained a temporary advantage, but not enough to save them; and with a few more judicious plays the reds drove the ball between the enemy's pennants, in some three minutes.

There was a very slight applause from a few gloved hands; the brass instruments blared again; and after a six minutes' interval the second game opened. Both this and the third went, like the first, against Thorburn, although his men performed some excellent feats. Once, the ball was driven out of bounds, and a remarkably correct young man, who had Miss Loyall on the box with him, ordered his groom to throw the small object of contention back; whereupon the players began to whack at it fiercely, until Colonel Clancy, who was acting as umpire, stopped them, and riding down to the boundary rope called out to the correct young man: "Don't you know any better than to throw the ball in like that?"

"Oh — aw, beg pahdon," said the culprit; and his accent was received as making entire amends.

"It strikes me," said Oliphant to the ladies, "that that's rather rough — addressing a gentleman in that style."

"Oh, no," Josephine assured him. "They have to be very strict. Why, they won't let anybody go inside the ropes, whatever happens."

Oliphant had dismounted, and stood beside the carriage, so as to get a nearer view. He also had a better view of Octavia and Josephine, who were remarkably effective that day; the former sitting beneath a small gold and violet dome of parasol, through which the light streamed softly, and Josephine receiving a peculiar glory from her crimson shelter.

In the fourth game a prolonged struggle began. It would have decided the day, if it had gone for the reds; but fortunately Thorburn had reserved his best pony until now, and in his desperate efforts to turn the tide, his blue and white shirt, his sunburned face and amber hair, seemed to be in all parts of the field at once. The crisis came when Richards, of the reds, delivered a clever blow from under his pony, and sent the ball rattling towards the blue flags, amid a good deal of applause. Thorburn darted after it like lightning, with both sides in full chase; then, with a neat back stroke, he reversed its direction, whirled around, and carried the crowd with him. Young Chiseling, however, of De Peyster's party, had hung back to keep the red goal; and seeing the ball go free, a little on one side, he bore down to strike it. Thorburn quickly noticed this move, and had already urged his pony with nervous leaps towards the same spot. He came shooting by, only a few yards from where Oliphant stood; and the next instant the two riders had clashed together and were thrown. They lay upon the grass slightly stunned, but the astonishing thing about the accident was that the two ponies had straddled: Thorburn's, his fore feet forced up into the air by the shock, had attempted to leap over Chiseling's, but had been unable to carry his hind legs clear, and so remained caught, with two hoofs on the ground.

There were ineffectual little shrieks from some of the ladies, and Clancy shouted, "Pull them apart, before they get to kicking!"

But he himself reined in at a safe distance, and the

players were gyrating in a knot, close to the red goal, wholly absorbed. Chiseling rose and walked off with a false and dazed attempt at self-possession, but Thorburn could do no more than sit up. The ponies were restive. Without stopping to reflect, Oliphant bent under the rope and rushed out to the point of danger.

"Get off the field!" thundered the umpire. The onlookers echoed him with warning shouts and murmurs. But Oliphant paid no attention: his blood was up. He grasped Thorburn's pony by the bridle, pulled with all his force, and compelled him to spring. This freed the animal; the other, turning sharply, trotted away and was caught by Clancy. The next thing was to lift Thorburn, who was soon able to move towards the tent: at the same moment, luckily, the ball was driven through by the blues, who thus retrieved their honor.

A double demonstration of approval greeted these performances; for, although Oliphant promptly retired to his previous obscurity, he was received with the warmest acknowledgments. There was quite a general clapping of hands in the neighborhood of Mrs. Gifford's carriage; and even Clancy came cantering in pursuit, to thank Oliphant for his service, while warning him that the interference was against all rules of the game. Atlee and Roger Deering, who were not far away, hastened up, to congratulate the hero of the hour. "By Jove, you know," said Atlee, glassing him all over, "it was — er — 'm — really fine, you know."

"Atlee means you're A 1," Roger remarked, grinning, and shaking his cousin's hand.

All this was nothing to Oliphant, compared with the homage that Octavia bestowed upon him. She gave him the full depth of her eyes, and smiled entrancingly as she said, "Bravo, Mr. Oliphant! I'm really proud of you; and I'm so glad you came with us, because we can share in your glory."

Josephine said nothing, but she, too, smiled; and there was a quality in her long, slow, fascinating look that penetrated Oliphant, — stirred him in fact so profoundly that he experienced something like alarm. Was it involuntary with her, or did it have a meaning?

Thorburn was not seriously hurt, but he found himself unable to sit his horse firmly, and had suffered a sprain in one wrist; accordingly, it was impossible to go on with the games. Octavia and Josephine took pains to drive over to the tent and inquire about his injuries, with a captivating appearance of being agitated; and yet Oliphant could see that he himself, although he had not undergone the slightest damage, was an object of far more interest to them. The flattery was like a bath of perfumes to him; no sort of discontent could trouble him now; he wished that he might go on living, for the rest of his term, in Newport and in the sight of Octavia. He drove with the ladies, and then stopped at High Lawn a few minutes, before leaving them. Josephine at first disappeared, giving him an opportunity to speak with Octavia alone; and he improved it by telling her the singular episode with Vivian Ware, which it seems that Justin had recounted to him.

"You observed her at the grounds, didn't you," he

asked, "riding with the count? She means to discipline our young friend, I judge."

"That is, torture him," said Octavia, with compassionate warmth. "It's too bad — too bad! Mr. Oliphant," she added, utilizing all the charm of her most confiding manner, "we must bring those two young people together — you and I!"

"With all my heart," he said, stumbling over the word, and wondered why she did not think that they themselves might also be brought together.

Josephine then came back; to whom, since she was about departing for Jamestown, he made his farewell. "Good-by," she responded, as she let her hand sink into his. "If you haven't been to Conanicut, you must come over and see us. My father, I'm sure, would be glad to meet you."

Again he felt the power of her steady and controlling gaze, to which Octavia was not blind, either; for Oliphant, who had the temerity to possess intuitions as quick as a woman's, saw that Octavia did not approve of the fascination her friend was deploying for his benefit. Well, he rather liked this: it was one more drop of flattery.

The days that followed gave him many meetings with Octavia — at dinners, at dances, at picnics of a stately, champagne-flavored kind near Paradise, or among the beeches and box-hedges and bay-bushes of the Glen, with its idle, mossy old grist-mill. He also came once or twice to High Lawn. Having made acquaintance with some delightful people who lived in a great house on Ocean Avenue, out of the Newport whirl, he found himself one of a party invited to spend a day there; and, Octavia being present, he strayed with her down a path in the rock, which stopped at the sheer edge of an undermined point, called by a picturesque terrorism The Pirate's Cave. Here they were invisible to the rest of the company. There had been a mirage all the morning, which threw Block Island up on the horizon as an inverted shape of towering sandy-tinted cliffs, in which the sails of becalmed ships made vertical white rifts; and this dim vision had haunted Oliphant with a hint of expectancy. But now it had vanished; and the sea, from being green compared with the sky, or pale blue beside the grass, was a deep blue everywhere.

"A change of color is an event here," said Oliphant. "It seems almost to change one's own mood."

"What *is* your mood, then?" asked Octavia.

"I could hardly tell you," he answered. "A while ago I was looking forward; and now I'm retrospective."

"Ah," said she, with a little frown, "it isn't good to be thinking of your past."

"I'm not: I'm thinking of yours!"

"Why?"

"Because that is where you seem to keep yourself. I continually catch a look in your eye which shows that you are wandering there. Why don't you live in the present?"

"But what is the present?" she replied. "Doesn't it dissolve at the touch of a memory or a hope — the past or the future?"

"I wish it could," he exclaimed fervently, "at the touch of a hope!"

A huge wave rolled into the cavern, as he spoke, and exploded there with a muffled sound like a knell.

"You're dissatisfied, then, with things as they are?"

"In one sense, very much so; in another, not at all. But I can imagine something better."

"There's where we differ," Octavia rejoined. "I'm very well content now; but my past was so complete and so sunny that there could hardly be any thing better."

"Well, you've heard me hint often enough that mine was a dreary failure. I gave my life up to one woman, and "— He checked himself, promptly.

"Yes," said Octavia; "it seems as if one had to be punished for too absolute a surrender. I gave myself up, too: I was happy, as I've said, but — that letter, Mr. Oliphant, that letter! That has been my punishment." It was the first time she had openly referred to it since the evening at Mrs. Ware's. "I should not say this to you," she added, "except that you have spoken frankly to *me*."

"I understand," he answered, appreciatively, more and more drawn on to speak from his heart. "But if it is possible for even the happiest career to be shadowed by a little thing, why should people let one experience settle the problem? Isn't it permitted to try again?"

"No, no!" she cried, in strange, unforeseen excitement. "You mustn't say that, Mr. Oliphant. It's sacrilege!"

And as she turned upon him, he felt the flame of her resentment; but he answered quietly: "You ought to be more indulgent to poor, irrepressible human nature. It has been ascertained that hope, like truth, when crushed, granulated, or powdered, will rise again."

She laughed faintly, and for a brief space they sat gazing out upon the waters, which passing clouds had suddenly softened to gray, seamed with many creeping wave-lines; a blind-looking ocean, yet watchful, as if waiting and preparing for some particular event. Then Octavia's glance came back to Oliphant, who in his gray suit appeared like a part of the lichened rock against which he was propped; his face, too, like the sea's, patient, prepared, but stronger.

There was a complete transformation in her when she resumed the talk. "Do you believe," she dreamily inquired, "that if a true love has once been given, it can ever be given again, — the same kind, I mean."

The hollow echo of an inrolling wave once more resounded upon their ears. "Perhaps not the same," Oliphant returned; "but there's always a question as to which is the best kind. It's a hard lesson to learn that the first conception, however exalted, may not be the wisest."

Octavia had a secret sense that there had been a lack in her first love; it had not welded into itself the substance of sorrow. Perhaps the love which should exist in spite of disappointment or doubt was the better developed sort — as shadows prove an object to be rounded. Fortifying herself against this suspicion, she said, "Love is a mistake, and marriage is a mistake, I fear. Looking back upon it, from our point of view, as something which is over for us, doesn't it strike you as strange that we should all be brought up to expect success in a matter so difficult? People ought to look to friendship, instead, which is the most unselfish affection."

"I doubt that. But as for friendship, I thought it was exhausted, too, until I met you, Mrs. Gifford. I fancied my life was a desert, and that my heart was turned to stone; but all at once, here's a fresh fountain springing out of the rock."

"Be careful!" Octavia interposed. "You're growing poetic, and you must remember we've reached the age of prose."

"Well, even prose will do for expressing belief. I wish you would believe, Mrs. Gifford."

"In what?"

"In the possibilities of the future."

She let her parasol droop, saying with dejection, "I should be glad if there were any such buoyancy in me. But hope and happiness have gone, Mr. Oliphant. See how Justin and Vivian, who really have any quantity of faith, assume to be sceptical; while I, who am a sceptic, do my best to believe, and can't."

"Didn't you say, though, a few minutes since, that you were content?"

"That was a conventional statement, a comparative one: I'm giving you the *un*conventional truth, now. Indeed, I shall never be contented again."

Oliphant rose to his feet, and stood before her on

the narrow ledge. Behind him was the slowly chafing sea; a light wind brought up the scent of shell and weed; the tide boomed sullenly in the deep recesses. There was Octavia, crouched against the granite wall, like another Andromeda, and Oliphant wished that he were Perseus.

"I shall never be content, myself," he said, with his hand on the iron rail along the verge, "except in one event."

A sparkle came from her eyes, rapid and keen as the light from her diamonds. "What one thing could have so much power?" she asked, with a half-tremulous smile that disintegrated his calmness.

"To see you happy," he exclaimed, "and to have some share in making you so!"

For an instant, Octavia was dismayed. Her hand, with jewelled rings upon it, sought the rough stone surface, for aid in rising; but Oliphant was quick to lend her his help, and she accepted it.

"You are very kind, to care so much about it," she said. "But are you not caring *too* much? Let me warn you in time." She spoke in haste, uneasily; yet all the while a subtle pleasure played around her lips, intoxicating Oliphant with the conviction that she did not really wish to repel him.

"No, no, Mrs. Gifford; I can't heed any warning; I can't take one. We have been thrown together strangely, by a fate that we couldn't control. Do you suppose I can control my interest in you, either? And would you be willing to take from me the one thing that makes life valuable to me now?"

"How can I take that away?" she asked, in a whisper; but he could hear it through the beating of the breeze.

"By denying me your companionship," he returned earnestly. "I want to be near you constantly, to do something for you; to be your reliance."

"Oh, it's impossible," murmured Octavia, shrinking slightly towards the high rock. "How can you expect that, Mr. Oliphant? What are you dreaming of?"

"Ah, if that's the way it strikes you," said Oliphant, "it is all useless; yes, it's only a dream, then! You need nothing; you are really happy enough, and my wish is a selfish one."

She made the slightest perceptible gesture of remonstrance, and seemed impelled to start towards him. "It is not selfish," said she, in melting tones. "I thank you for your generous feeling; indeed, I do. But you know people can't form such companionships: there is no room in this world for the finest impulses."

Scintillant reflections from the water chased each other over the granite surface behind Octavia, and dazzled Oliphant; but the conflicting moods that flitted across her face dazzled and bewildered him still more. She seemed alternately a coy girl unwilling to be won; a woman recognizing with devout joy the dawn of love; a shape of distant perfection, wholly unattainable. Through it all, he held to the one thought that he desired her more than any thing on earth, and, however mad the scheme, was determined to win her.

"You told me," he said, growing bold as he grew

agitated, "that friendship is the best affection. But if there's no place for our friendship, there may be for something else."

Octavia started, but she made no sharp protest. Instead, she gazed at him meditatively for a moment, and he discerned in her large inquiring eyes a womanly sense of the devotion which he offered — a tenderness blended with pity and pride. She, however, raised one finger to her lips in admonition.

"It's time for us to be interrupted, Mr. Oliphant, if you have come to that. Shall we interrupt ourselves?"

"Are you going to joke me?" he asked, with pain. "Surely you see how much in earnest I am. You will listen and consider?"

She detected the transfiguring light upon his features, as he leaned nearer towards her. "I — I didn't mean to joke," she said, with seductive contrition. Oliphant believed then that she would yield to his entreaty that she should hear him. Suddenly there came a shock of change; apprehension seemed to have assailed her; she clasped her hands, and cried out, "No, I cannot listen! Don't ask me to, — don't ask me."

An undertone as of sobbing rang in that cry, and Oliphant's forehead grew white and wrinkled with anxiety. "Why do you look at me so, Mrs. Gifford? What have I done?"

"Look? How am I looking?"

"You seem angry, as well as pained. I should think that you hated and despised me for this."

At that instant a gull came wheeling through the air above them, with a weird, vibrating scream; and the hollow rock was filled again with the baffled roar of a retreating billow.

Octavia's eyes fell, and she said very slowly, "No, I do not hate you."

He recovered hope at once. "Then you forgive me," he concluded buoyantly; "and you will let me speak, some time. Will you think of what I have said?"

The wildness of her outburst had died away, and the indescribable smile mingled of coquetry and undisguised emotion, which Oliphant had already noticed, resumed its sway, as she answered: "At least, I sha'n't be likely to forget it."

X.

YOUNG THORBURN AND OLD THORBURN.

PERRY discovered that there were compensations for his accident on the polo-field, which would almost have persuaded him to undergo another like it. He made a languid state progress from his father's enormous villa on the Cliffs to the Casino, the Club, the houses of his friends; carrying his arm in a sling, and accepting the solicitude, the admiration, and the fervent good wishes of many beautiful young ladies and sweetly judicious mammas. Not a bad fellow was this Perry, by nature; but he had of course been spoiled as a boy, and it was quite delightful to him to find that he could now indulge himself with a complete relapse into unreasonableness, on the excuse of an injured arm. He enjoyed the affectionate abasement of his mother and the uncouth tenderness of his father, both of whom suffered from a belief (and yet were pleased by it) that they did not come up to his standard. He also enjoyed being taken out on the avenue by some of the best "whips" among the ladies, and resigning himself like a wounded veteran to their graceful management of the reins. Frequently he sailed over to Jamestown, to call on Josephine; and as the Thorburns had brought no yacht to Newport, Raish Porter quickly saw the advantage of placing his own boat at Perry's disposal. All this time, however, Perry tortured his household with the most capricious moods, and took especial pains to make Quisbrough the victim of his pseudo-invalidism.

Quisbrough still exercised a feeble tutorial function, although Perry had reached the age of twenty-four. The young man had never been to college. As Quisbrough once confidentially remarked, "At first, owing to Perry's want of appreciation for the requirements, Harvard wouldn't admit him; and afterwards, in retaliation, he refused to admit Harvard." He was understood to be pursuing advanced studies in private, and even entertained notions of astonishing the world, some day; but his instructor really had little to do, beyond certain duties as secretary to Thorburn senior and the submitting himself to Perry's persecutions. He was obliged to go in the yacht to Jamestown, remaining fixed on board while the autocrat spent an hour or two with Josephine; and afterwards he had to listen to his charge's laudations of that young woman, his sentimental anxieties, and his peevish dissatisfaction because both his father and Mr. Hobart opposed a union with her: the former for the reason that he wanted his vast fortune to be joined, through his son's marriage, with some other immense accumulation; while Mr. Hobart strenuously demurred at the idea of losing his daughter's care and companionship, in his increasing age and ill-health.

Returning from one of these trips, Perry insisted

upon stretching himself, propped by a pillow, on a sofa in his father's library, a long and wide, low-studded apartment, fitted up with much grandeur of dark-hued wood, rows of elegant, unread books in solid cases — which, viewing their dead and useless contents, one might have considered the catacombs of literature — and as many other appliances for display as the architect and furnisher had allowed. The windows were of plain glass, but were heavily leaded in a pattern somewhat resembling a spider-web. The proprietor of this lordly place was seated at an immense desk — the high altar of his religion — bestowed in a capacious alcove; one that could be shut off at will from the main apartment, and had a vaulted ceiling on which the web design re-appeared. He was extracting benefit from his seaside leisure by reading some cipher despatches which had just come from New York through his private wire. The click of the instrument, in charge of a private operator, could be heard through an open door leading from the library; and there was so much privacy altogether about the arrangement that to any one but Perry it would have been sacred. The only tribute, however, that he paid to the established cult was the incense of a cigar which he proceeded to light.

"Why do you come in here, boy?" asked his father, turning his head for an instant towards Perry. Thorburn was so heavy a man, his head was so cumbrous, that he seemed hardly capable of looking *at* any one; but the aspect of shrewd and searching intelligence marked upon the bulky, almost brutish features was distinct, and became, by contrast with their dull weight, rather unpleasant — in fact, terrifying at times, like the sudden projection of a tree or a rock at night, which transiently takes on the appearance of a monster's head. "Haven't you got rooms enough of your own?" he continued. "I'm busy."

"That's the reason I came," said his son. "I like to see you doing business."

Old Thorburn settled himself into his former position, as a sign of his displeasure, and was soon absorbed again. Perry, having waited for this, resumed: "Besides, I've got something to speak about."

"Can't hear it," said his father, without moving.

"Well, it's just as you like," Perry answered, imperturbably. "I thought it would be fair to tell you, but I'll go ahead any way, without consulting you."

"What is it?" Mr. Thorburn asked, in a voice as heavy as his features, — as heavy as a sponge full of water. "Business?"

"No. More important than that. I'm going to marry Josephine Hobart."

"What!" exclaimed Mr. Thorburn, dropping his papers and facing round. "After my stating expressly that I disapprove of it?" He rose, walked across the room, and closed the door of the private telegraph-office. "Have you spoken to her?"

"No," said Perry, in a very comfortable manner, with his cigar in his mouth. "But I'm going to, soon."

At this point, Mr. Thorburn noticed that Quisbrough had remained in the room. "You may leave us," he said to the tutor-secretary. "This is private," and with a short, arbitrary gesture, he indicated the surroundings, himself, and Perry.

But Perry, seeing an opportunity to embarrass Quisbrough, said: "No, Quiz, I'd rather have you stay. He knows all about it," he added, to his father.

Quisbrough, without looking at either of them, continued the perusal of a small book which he had taken from his pocket, and did not move.

"Very well, sir," continued Thorburn, addressing Perry, "let us have an explanation. You must be crazy! Why, you haven't finished your education yet."

"No, I haven't," the young man returned; "but, for all that, I know a good deal more than you do about some things."

Quisbrough, leaning against the base of a book-case, glanced up with a little quirk in his thick beard, that apparently resulted from a smile. "Perry flatters me," he observed, "beyond my deserts."

"You know a lot more about infernal impudence," Thorburn proceeded, to his only child, "than I could afford at your age; and that's about all you *have* learned. It's pretty near time for me to give you a lesso or two myself, and I'm damned if I don't do it."

The heir of the estate smiled blandly, and leaned back on his pillow. "There," said he, "is where you're considerably off your chump, if you think you can teach me. I don't see the use of getting excited: I only thought it would make things pleasanter and smoother if I gave you fair notice that I'm going to marry Josephine; and that's all there is to it."

Old Thorburn glowered at him for a moment. The millionnaire had a big face, with long and copious side-whiskers that enclosed a huge shaven area about the coarsely moulded lips and chin; and the big eyes above his well-fed and well-wined cheeks disclosed, even in his genial moments, a semi-indignant expression, as if they were outraged by the unfortunate spectacle of the lower face over which they were compelled to take their observations. At present they were more indignant than usual. "Look here, Perry," he inquired finally, "do you suppose I'm going to submit to this? Do you really mean to tell me that without resources of your own — no business, no opportunities — nothing but the hundred thousand or so that I've given you, you're going to undertake a marriage against my will? You can't be such a fool!"

Perry exhaled a meditative wreath of smoke. "Well," he replied, gently, "I should relax my features; I should murmur ever so sweetly."

"What does the cub mean," Thorburn asked, turning helplessly to Quisbrough, "by those idiotic phrases? Does he mean yes or no?"

"On the whole," said Quisbrough gravely, "I should say he meant yes."

"Right you are," declared Perry, nodding his head.

"Then, all I've got to say," his father exclaimed, growing redder in the face and squaring his big body at the reclining athlete, "is this: I forbid it! I won't have it, I tell you! And I'll find ways to stop it, if I want; you may be sure of that. Why, old Hobart is opposed to it, too — he told me so; and I'll make it for his interest to be still more opposed. Or if that won't do, I'll buy the girl off, herself."

Perry leaped from the couch at one bound. "Stop that, sir!" he cried. "There's one thing you can't do, any way; and that is, insult the lady I mean to marry. By thunder, if it comes to that, I walk straight out of this house and stay out. Take your choice." In his excitement, he tore the lame arm free from its bandage.

The magnate was cowed, for an instant. The owner of railroads and parts of railroads and masses of the national debt; the great operator in stocks; the man who had bought up a line of Newport steamers merely as a diversion, and was running them in sumptuous style, with bands of music to give a concert on every trip; the owner of sundry revered trotting-horses; the dealer in legislatures below par;—this individual, I say, was frightened by a few manly words from his useless and indolent son. Nevertheless, he growled, after a pause, though not without a strain of conciliation in the gruff, guttural speech: "It's strange that I can't have my own way in a matter like this—a matter right in my own family. I've bought things a deuced sight more important than the obedience of a boy or the refusal of a girl." Here a humorous contraction of the muscles rolled his lips back in a grim smile. "But filial affection, I suppose, is a luxury that I ought to appreciate, even if I get it for nothing." He was pleased with his sarcasm, but, growing angry again, he continued: "All the same, I won't have this thing. Mind now I'm opposed to it, first and last;

and if you persist, I'll disinherit you — at least for your mother's life — and cut you down to the lowest figure, any way you can fix it."

"Oh, I know you're a hard customer, when you've made your mouth up," said Perry, returning to slang. This indirect allusion to the unfortunate feature in his father's physiognomy was by no means soothing. "Still, I've got some capacity, too, for going ahead, when I want to. I'm not afraid."

"Will you allow me one word?" Quisbrough now interposed, seemingly fatigued to the point of somnolence. "It strikes me, Mr. Thorburn, that you're forgetting just for the moment our American principles of free action, and so forth. What you propose to do would be all very well in the old country, but it doesn't suit the genius of our institutions. You see, you haven't got any background for it."

"Background!" roared Thorburn. "What do you call this?" He waved his arm, and as it were swept the whole vista of the opulent room at his critic: the panelled wood ceiling, the luxurious chairs, the sham old armor, and the spider-web tracery of the leaded windows. "What do you call my business interests? If all that isn't background enough, I don't know where you'll find it."

"It's as good as possible, in its way," said the secretary, whose sedate manner of treating the question in a philosophic mood filled Perry with satirical joy; "but what I refer to is the social system of the country. We need two or three centuries of a well-defined money aristocracy, with entail and a fixed principle of parental authority, before a man can expect to control his son's matrimonial choice."

Thorburn did not fail to see that his adroit employee, although assuming the position of a futile theorizer, had really opened for him the best way out of the dispute. Besides, he was rapidly sketching, in the close-barred retirement of his own mind, where there was neither secretary nor private wire, a delectable scheme for impressing his unruly offspring, and getting him into a "tight place;" and, sharp though his irritation remained, the first move in that scheme must, he was aware, be to conciliate Perry.

He affected to ponder Quisbrough's words. "Perhaps you are right," he said, throwing into his reply a careful reluctance. "If I wanted any traditions badly enough, I guess I could make 'em for myself; still, you may be right, Quisbrough. It may be better to float with the current in this particular case. Well, Perry, my boy,"— his demeanor softened into something like that of a trained bear, — "I don't like it, but I shall try to make the best of it, if it's bound to happen. 'First catch your hare,' though: you've got to get the young lady's consent."

"I'll attend to that," replied the other, serenely.

"Then suppose we drop the subject. I shall have something to say to you by and by; some hints that may be useful. But not now: I'm busy." Saying which, Thorburn reseated himself at his desk.

"All right. Come along, Quiz," said Perry. "I want you to fix up this sling for me." He began chuckling, after they left the room. "By Jove, the old man was bowled over pretty easily, eh? Hadn't any idea he'd give in. Now we've got to settle Hobart, and I don't see how to do it. Do you?"

His companion professed a total inability to assist, but at once began to cogitate upon methods of doing so. It was not long before circumstances placed in his hands a complete outline of the measures to be adopted. Raish Porter, having lent his yacht to Perry for the excursions to Jamestown, found opportunities to carry him off now and then, on brief cruises up the bay or along the outer shore; and in the course of these miniature voyages he allowed particulars to be drawn from him respecting the important enterprises of the Orbicular Manufacturing Company. With the diffidence of a man who is sure in the ownership of a property that must naturally excite the envy of others, he let fall significant items about the new patents for cotton-roving machines which he controlled; he also alluded to valuable railroad appliances to be produced by the Orbicular Company, the monopoly of which alone would bring in a princely revenue. By and by he allowed him to learn that Mr. Hobart was a heavy investor in the concern; a fact which stimulated Perry's attention to a wonderful degree.

"I presume," said Raish heartily, — "since it's no secret. — that you know of the attacks which have been made on the company and myself, during the last few weeks. They were started by one of those blackmailing commercial papers — no account — and have been taken up by a few others. But look at the great dailies. The Luminary, of course, is down on us —

down on every thing, if it thinks there's half a chance. The Trumpeter writes one way first, and then the other, so's to be 'independent.' But all the rest steer clear, and there hasn't been a particle of evidence produced yet. The best answer to these slanders is the big factory we're putting up out in Jersey: it'll cost us a quarter of a million. You can't imagine, though, how annoying this irresponsible onslaught is. Some of the best men are stockholders, but we have really been slightly impeded by this thing; capital, you know, is so sensitive. Still, you remember, it has been said that ' half the failures in life arise from pulling in one's horse as he is leaping; ' and I don't propose to pull mine in just now. Not by a long sight!" Raish laughed with great good cheer, in conclusion.

Quisbrough waited for Perry to broach the topic, when they were alone, and then he gradually admitted, with an apologetic air, that since Porter was evidently prepared to accept a new subscriber for Orbicular stock, and also had great influence with Hobart, his energies might be enlisted to break down the old gentleman's objection to the match with Josephine, if Perry should put money into the new company. Such a manœuvre strongly commended itself to the millionnaire's son, who fancied that he saw in it the means of outwitting his father, and at the same time conducting a profitable business operation for himself. Within a day or two, accordingly, he arrived at an understanding with Porter, and agreed to take a large number of shares in the Orbicular.

Meanwhile, he crossed the bay again, to see Josephine. She was staying with her father at a barren old farm-house, which stood out in the green fields, surrounded by a few stunted trees; and as Perry approached, he found the small covered piazza in sole possession of the old gentleman, assisted by a brood of dauntless chickens who were wandering all over it. "What a frightful place for her to be in!" thought the gallant suitor, as he had often thought before.

Small Mr. Hobart, white-bearded, red-nosed, fussy, laid down his paper, and presented to the suitor a countenance barred by a pair of gold spectacles, which appeared to restrain and imprison the choleric wearer, compelling him to observe an artificial civility. He greeted Perry much more cordially than usual. "Glad to see you," he said. "It shows you have some sense, to get away occasionally from that ridiculous merry-go-round on the other side of the water, and come over here. I've heard some news about you, too: it seems you're beginning to make a business man of yourself."

Perry blushed, as well as he could with his sunburned complexion; in part from modesty, but still more from pride at the first sign of success attending his machination.

"Well, yes," he said, "I've been talking with Mr. Porter a little about your new company. It's a good thing, isn't it?"

"Splendid, sir!" exclaimed Mr. Hobart, in a cracked voice, taking a pull at the short brier pipe he was smoking. "You can't do better, as a beginning. Lucky chance for you: there ain't many men Porter would think of letting in; but I'm glad he's inclined to give you a block, I swear. You didn't come here to talk business, though," the retired merchant continued, giving a wretched imitation of hilarity in the form of a shattered laugh. "Josie isn't in the house; she's just walked up the road, there. I guess you'll overtake her, though, if you follow."

And Perry did overtake her. Exactly what occurred need not be recited here in detail; but half an hour later, Quisbrough beheld his overgrown pupil striding down to the water's edge at an impatient pace. He came out in a boat to the yacht, and boarded her without uttering a syllable; he maintained a rigorous silence, in fact, all the way home. But it was not the silence of satisfaction; and at length scattered ejaculations, like the first drops of a storm, began to fall upon Quisbrough, making known to him the result of the interview. Josephine had not refused Perry; but she had put him off, had asked him to wait. Over and over there recurred to his mind with galling persistence the excuses, the delays, the remonstrances, she had made.

"I am almost sure of gaining your father over," he had said; "and, even without that, I should still ask you to marry me. I want to take you away from this broken-up, unhappy sort of life you lead with him, and to place you where you belong. Fortunately, I shall have all the means for giving you surroundings that would be worthy of you, Josephine. It will be pleasure enough for my whole life, only to do that. But if I were miserably poor, I should love you just the same, and have just the same ambition for you. Is that nothing to you?"

"Ah no, no; you do really love me, I am certain," she replied, regarding him calmly, dreamily, with her dark, restful eyes; "and to know it, I will tell you fairly, is a great deal to me, whether I will or not. But " —

"Oh, you mean you can't return my sentiments," he interrupted, hotly. "Is that it?"

"Don't force me to say so, Mr. Thorburn," she admonished him. Her bearing was as serene, as unaffected and yet queenly, standing there with one elbow leaned on the roadside stone-wall, and with open, wind-swept fields stretching out on every side, as it would have been if they had met in the most formal drawing-room of Newport.

"I only want to know the hard fact," he declared, obstinately. "Whatever it may be, I warn you I shall try to overcome it: I can't help trying. But only let me know. Oh!" he suddenly exclaimed, clapping one hand to his temple with unmerciful sharpness. "Perhaps that's it, but I never thought of it. I might have known, though: you — you are thinking of some one else!"

Josephine desisted from her unfaltering gaze, and the long eyelashes swept downward as she answered, almost repeating her former appeal, "Don't ask me. I can't say that, either."

"Then, if it isn't so," he implored, "what is the reason? What can be the difficulty?"

She bent her glance, as it happened, towards the bay; she turned towards the spot where distant Newport lay in a confused mass of huddled gray roofs and spires on the dim opposite shore. There was a strange expectancy in her mein, as if she awaited an impossible relief from that quarter. "Mr. Thorburn," she said, in honest distress, "I beg you won't go on. I can't explain; truly, I can't. I respect your devotion and your kindness, and I don't want to inflict any hurt upon you; but oh, indeed, you mustn't ask me any more!"

Nothing had availed to wring from her any utterance more satisfactory than this; and so poor Perry, who had counted with such assurance upon his factitious advantages and his unqualified affection, was left to reconcile himself to the baffling situation as well or ill as he could. He promptly adopted the expedient of becoming reckless. As may well be guessed, nothing was revealed to his father concerning the set-back he had encountered; but the wily old manipulator noted in him signs of a desperation, which, however, was still temperate, if one may say so. Perry avoided the society of ladies, now, and hung about the clubs, drinking and smoking a good deal; he also dropped in at the secret and luxurious gambling-place, politely supposed not to exist, where Stillman Ware often sought diversion. One day old Thorburn summoned him, being ready to ignite the train he had laid.

"I see you are restless," he said, "and I think I can guess why. Of course it's natural you should feel the responsibilities of the line you are taking. You need more money than you've got, and you don't know how to make it."

"No, I suppose I don't know much about that,"

said Perry, amused to think what a surprise he would give the old gentleman with his manufacturing-stock, by and by.

"Well, this is what I referred to, the other day — hints I wanted to give. You haven't considered my feelings nor obeyed my wish about Miss Hobart; but I shall do you a good turn, notwithstanding. Do you know how Transcontinental Telegraph stands now?"

As this was one of the most uncertain among the great speculative stocks, Perry could not say precisely; and his father gave him the quotation. "My ticker," he said, "showed it at seventy-one and three-quarters, about ten minutes ago. I advise you to buy in for a rise." Thorburn was exceedingly amiable, at this moment, but contrived also to make his advice as impressive as a command.

"Is there going to be a 'deal'?" his son inquired, eying him intelligently.

"If there were," said his father, "it wouldn't do for me to tell you any thing about it. Now, I don't want you to ask questions: I only advise you to buy. After you have jumped in, you must rely on your own swimming. *I* sha'n't explain to you what you're to do; but I feel confident we shall see Transcontinental at ninety-five, or par, before many weeks are over. And by the way, my boy, don't mention this to any one, unless it be two or three of your intimate friends."

Perry was quite captivated by his father's conversion and kindness. He at once sent an order to Roger Deering, in New York, to make a considerable purchase of Transcontinental for his account. That proceeding was followed by a creditable impulse to show Raish some gratitude for his service with regard to Mr. Hobart; for although matters did not yet advance any farther in Perry's wooing of Josephine, Raish's arguments had been effectual at all events in gaining her father's assent. He had represented to Mr. Hobart that the cash assets, of which just then their company stood most indigently in need, would be furnished by young Thorburn, provided Josephine were not trammelled by parental opposition. Nothing could have been more natural than that, by way of returning this favor, Perry should have bethought him of imparting to Raish the priceless suggestion which his father had thrown out. To disregard a hint from this source would have seemed to Porter a folly for which he would never be able to pardon himself; moreover, the prospect of a swift and colossal profit was one that, in the temporary embarrassment of his manufacturing project, was peculiarly acceptable. He, too, began buying; and somehow many other people in Newport, in New York, in other cities, or in simple, uncovetous country regions, were seized with a like inspiration at the same time. They winged their way to the brokers for Transcontinental, even as bees fare to the garden for honey. As a consequence, the stock went up several points in a few days. Meanwhile, old Thorburn, to whose industry this cheering circumstance was due, continued to officiate at his altar-like desk in the little chancel or alcove off the library; and the tangled mouldings above his head continued to figure the meshes of a web. The special wire ran out from the house like a thread prolonged from those meshes; it tingled and grew alive with the quick, secret current of thought pulsating through it from the owner's brain; and the owner himself remained physically inert within, as deceptively quiet as if he had actually been an enlarged and improved species of spider watchfully presiding over those complicated filaments.

XI.

OLIPHANT, OCTAVIA, AND JOSEPHINE.

AT this time Oliphant felt all the romance of his youth returning to him. He was thoroughly and beyond help in love with Octavia; nothing that he could remember, nothing that he could fear or forecast, had any power to restrain him from his one great hope of making her his wife. When he recalled his first passion for Alice Davenant — which had thus far been the single mastering emotion of his life-time — it was only to wonder at the dim insubstantiality into which it now faded: he was completely puzzled, and remained unable to reconcile the two sentiments. Invariably he came back to the simple truth that it was Octavia to whom he looked for a realization of perfect happiness; she it was for whom he wished to exist. Certainly, he was troubled by a lingering tradition of loyalty to Alice; and the belief that Octavia also was haunted by a theory of dedicating herself forever to her lost husband constantly intervened, to make him hesitate about bringing his hopes to another and a final test. But then, too. the consideration would come up that Alice, so far as the evidence went, had not found in him the adequate companion that, for some reason, we human beings believe ourselves entitled to. Had she, by a sardonic coincidence, made a fatal error in refusing Gifford; while he, too late, had met this appointed counterpart in Octavia? The conflict between these doubts and the one certainty did not, as we should at first imagine, depress him. No; it stimulated him; the tide of vitality flowed stronger and more buoyant in him on account of them. At moments he suffered intensely, but he rejoiced in his suffering. At other times his spirits rose to a point of volatile gayety which they had not attained in years. He had rapidly gained standing in the most attractive and well-founded society of the town, as a favorite against whom no objection was heard; and to escape the anxieties he felt respecting his fate with Octavia, he insensibly gave himself up more and more to the intoxicating festivities which offered on every side. He had been in the deep places of sorrow long enough; surely it was permissible for him to float on the surface, now, as much as he liked. The object of Newport was pleasure, and pleasure suited him perfectly. And so he came into a better sympathy with the so-called frivolous world than he had ever experienced until then.

"Yes," he replied to one of Raish's burly strictures, "fashionable life here is hollow; but since all of us are more or less hollow, why object to that? Fashion is not the fruit, it's merely the passing flower, of human desires; and the special beauty of a flower is that it *isn't* solid."

Mary Deering asked him if he was not convinced that she had done wisely in counselling him to come thither, and he said vigorously: "Indeed you did! Do you know how it strikes me? I feel as if I were one of those figures on a drop-curtain. No matter what tragedies have happened, or are to come, on the stage, the drop-curtain population is always serene and soothing, and lives in a softly colored landscape. It's so here, too."

It was while Perry was still laboring under depression that Oliphant strolled one day into the billiard-room of the old Club, and found him there. Perry was playing with De Peyster; and, although it was early in the afternoon, he had just ordered a second bottle of champagne when our friend entered. "Here, I'll pay up now," he said to the waiter. "How much is it?" And he pulled out from his trousers-pocket a handkerchief, which dragged with it gold and silver pieces that fell on the floor. Without noticing this mishap, he dived into his pocket again, and produced a handful of the precious metals, while the waiter was collecting the crumbs of wealth already fallen. In fact, every thing he did betrayed a disdainful heat of temper. He stalked around the table as if it were something he had a contempt for; he spoke little with De Peyster; and he didn't recognize the existence of Quisbrough, who sat in one of the cushioned chairs fixed in a row at the side of the room; except that now and then he sent him a glass of wine. The tutor always drank it in silence, and went on smoking cigarettes imperturbably, his face subdued to a self-contained, dryly sagacious expression. Oliphant took a place beside him. They had before now established a pleasant and easy-going acquaintance, and Quisbrough had shown a willingness to accept Oliphant on terms almost of intimacy, for he evidently trusted him.

"You are continuing your course of instruction, I see," Oliphant observed.

"Yes," said Quiz. "It's decidedly arduous. I have to cover so many branches. Just think of a man undertaking to be an Alma Mater, and all by himself! That's what I have to do. I'm a walking college, which has to go wherever Perry does; and, what's worse, I have to be professor at the same time. Just at present I'm occupying the chair of billiards, you notice. Very arduous, very!"

After a while, Perry continuing his proud moroseness, the two onlookers strayed out together on the roofless platform at the side of the club-house. "Your undergraduate seems to be in a troubled state of mind," said Oliphant.

"Yes; he's luxuriating in a sentiment, I believe," Quiz returned.

"My friend Porter has told me something about it," Oliphant at once explained. "He's an extraordinary fellow for finding out things. I infer that Perry has confided a good deal to him, and I knew already of the attachment to Miss Hobart. What a curious thing all this love-making is, and the misery people create for themselves out of it!"

"Very odd," Quiz agreed, with sedate humor. "It's not a part of the prescribed course for Perry — only an elective; but as he has chosen it, I've been obliged to read the subject up, and I don't mind saying that I fail to master it. If it's a science, it's the science of unreason; but if it's an art, it's the art of helpless nature. Then, there are the different conceptions of love in various ages and countries: no one can say exactly what the essence is, common to all the ideas of it. Nowadays we're governed mainly by what Hegel calls the Romantic view. Would you like to hear how he states it?" Straightway, Quiz hauled forth a note-book and began reading: " 'The highest phase of love is the devotion of the subject or person to an individual of the opposite sex,' — profound, isn't it? — ' the surrender of his independent consciousness, and of his individual, isolated being-for-himself, which feels itself to have become thoroughly penetrated with its own knowledge of itself, for the first time, in the consciousness of another.' Now, does that make it any clearer?" He went on mumbling out words like "abstract . . . concrete . . . individualized . . . my entire subjectivity," until Oliphant laughingly stopped him.

"That'll do for the philosophy of it," he said.

"Oh, well, I'm crammed with the poetry of the thing, too," responded Quiz, ruffling the leaves of his little book. "The sum and substance of the poetical doctrine is that the less you can tell why you love, and the more you can glory in your ignorance, the better. Turn to index of authors, under L. John Lilly: "Affection is a fire, which kindleth as well in the bramble as in the oak; and catcheth hold where it first lighteth, — not where it may best burn.' Under M., Milton, thusly : —

"'It is not virtue, wisdom, valor, wit,
Strength, comeliness of shape, or amplest merit,
That woman's love can win or long inherit.'

And, not to bore you, so it goes on; but they all agree that there's something very fine about love. It's a sort of superstition — like religion."

Oliphant became grave. "I've been a man of the world, Quisbrough," said he, "but I hold on to my religion, and it isn't superstitious; so I can't quite accept your remark. Love, like religion, appears to me to be a result of faith. Our belief in the good and noble traits of humanity is apt to be disappointed in most cases, and by the flaws and meannesses we discover in ourselves, too. But when a man falls in love, he concentrates his general belief in the fine qualities of mankind on one person; he has faith that she is mainly composed of those qualities; and that faith — as we see often enough — will carry him through life cheerfully, in face of the most glaring contradictions. Even when he detects the woman's faults, he is fond of them, almost proud of them, because — well, simply because he loves her."

"Ah, you see," Quisbrough retorted, "you come back, as I do, to the 'because,' which doesn't explain any thing. And as to your faith — there's so much selfishness, after all, in love! It's a mutual agreement to be kind and generous, and to believe, on the distinct ground that a full equivalent shall be given in return. You know how easily love turns to hate; well, that proves it to be selfish. But this is just the quality that makes it so delightful to people: the passion is merely selfishness in an etherealized form, which intoxicates the partaker, inverts his ideas, and makes him think — or her think — that this emotion which is dilating the bosom, and so on, is a magnanimous self-surrender."

"But aren't there instances of persons who love long after they have ceased to receive any return?"

"Yes; you're right; but they're rare, I imagine. Any way, that belongs to the higher branches: Perry will need a post-graduate course to get so far."

At this moment Mr. Farley Blazer appeared on the balcony. He liked to worry himself by coming down to Newport sometimes and living in a separate apartment, whence he could watch his wife following her path of glory by means of his wealth. On this occasion he was very much under the influence of liquor, and was humming a song, —

> "The last poor rat,
> Without a cravat;
> He had no coat,
> And a hole in that," —

which perhaps symbolized to him his own mental condition. He invited the two talkers to drink, but they declined; and, after a few companionable remarks of a luridly humorous nature, he withdrew his wild beard and dull eyes from their sight.

"There's an example, now," Quiz resumed. "That man still loves his wife, though she doesn't care a rap for him; and he's paying her the costly tribute of drinking himself to death, because there isn't any other way to show his regard."

Oliphant had a sudden thought of Roger Deering; for ugly rumors about Mary and Atlee had been flying rather thick of late. And then, passing from these two instances of damaged conjugal affection, his mind reverted to the milk-and-water of Hawkstane's kindness, which was now rapidly turning its current towards Tilly Blazer. How could that feeble sentiment be classed with Craig's devouring passion for Vivian? And then, again, could the name of love be applied to the instinctive calculations of the various smiling, talkative little rosebuds and the statelier belles of society, who were able to gauge their heart-throbs by a bank account and prospects of "position;" or to the moth-flights of Dana Sweetser?

"There are about as many degrees in these matters," he said, "as there are individuals. According to your notion, though, I suppose the giving of devotion with absolutely nothing in exchange would be the perfect phase of love."

"I should call it the highest," was Quisbrough's reply. "What is heroism but a generalized, intense love of others, who, perhaps, don't know that we exist? Men lay down their lives for total strangers whom they see in peril."

"But that's a case of honor, or duty, or enthusiasm. There's no passion in it; is there?"

"It strikes me there's passion of the finest kind in such deeds," Quisbrough declared. "If they're not prompted by a sublimated, unselfish power of love, I can see no motive in them at all."

"I never looked at it in that way," Oliphant said,

yieldingly. "But I shouldn't wonder if you had hit the truth. Of course love must be an idea, as well as a passion ; and probably most of us don't come within a thousand miles of comprehending the whole idea."

No doubt he meant what he said ; but, as he walked away from the club, he told himself that a man like Quisbrough could not really know any thing about it. His own love for Octavia, he was firmly convinced, rose to the highest mark : he knew that he would do any thing for her ; he would sacrifice himself for her, if need were ; and, should she be unwilling to share her life with him, he was still capable of making his own minister to hers wherever an opportunity offered That night he walked out towards her house. In the high slope of the roof one window was still glowing, which he tried to suppose was hers, at the same time that he argued against its being so. He wandered up and down the neighboring roads in the rich, soft silence, feeling the moist sea-breeze on his face, and gazing now and then at a bank of white, inchoate cloud-shapes that throbbed with a dim uncertainty of silver light above the tardy moon. Remote, intangible and fair as those, were the hopes that shone down into his midnight revery ; but he resolved soon to attempt to realize them.

He was to see Octavia the next day ; for they had made an appointment with Craig, who wanted them to hear him practise on the organ in the old church. Oliphant called for her at the hour agreed upon, and they drove to Trinity together. She was rather pale that morning ; the reason of which was that she had in fact been sitting up when Oliphant made his nocturnal reconnaissance, and had been thinking a good deal about him. He was sensible of a new reserve in her manner, which, instead of warning him away, drew him — he could not tell how — nearer, and thrilled him with a vague exultation. On the way she talked of nothing but Craig and Vivian, who were still at odds; and it seemed that Vivian had been doing all sorts of vexatious things to increase Justin's discouragement: she was flirting desperately, and defying the conventionalities more than ever. She had even committed the indiscretion of sharing in a game of polo played entirely by ladies, which had been conducted with great secrecy, but had nevertheless come to everybody's knowledge and been commented on severely.

"I have decided," said Oliphant, "to send Justin to Germany, and he will go before the season's out. We must get up a reconciliation by that time."

"Oh, yes; and sooner," Octavia rejoined. "I haven't yet told you how anxious Dana Sweetser is to have Justin give a concert for the Drainage Association. We'll persuade Vivian to get his consent. Won't that be nice? And do you know what else I've done? I'm afraid it shows dreadful duplicity in me, but I couldn't help it: I — I told her we were all going to be at the church to-day!"

Octavia looked at him (they were in the carriage) with mingled mischief and contrition, and the effect of her glance was greatly heightened by the bonnet she wore, which was made entirely of pansies, and crowned her with a simple grace worthy of some mythical wood-nymph. Were I to tell what Oliphant thought of this piece of head-gear, and how he worshipped it, I should make him appear ridiculous to every one excepting such ladies as may have had a bonnet just like it; but the alluring light in her eyes, the trustful reliance that he would respond to her mood, and her sunshiny liveliness — faintly shadowed always by that reserve I have mentioned — were of far more importance to him. What could all these mean, unless that she resented nothing of what he had said at the Pirate's Cave, and that she might be induced to listen to him again? And so, blithely and sympathetically, they entered the empty church, took places in one of the pews where they could see Justin as well as hear his playing, and had great enjoyment of the music together. It was delightful to know that one identical strain of harmony was sweeping through them both at the same time; and they exchanged many swift looks of approval and pleasure at particular passages. And then, as they were preparing to go away, Octavia, fancying that she heard a light step in the vestibule below, hurried to a window in the gallery. Justin was putting in the organ-stops; she beckoned Oliphant to come to her side; and, standing there, he saw Vivian in the path leading out of the old grave-yard. She had of course been listening, unseen, to the music. She happened to turn at the moment, glanced up, and saw them; and they hastily drew back, though not before Octavia had shaken her finger jestingly at her friend.

"You see, I knew what would be the effect of telling her," she whispered to Oliphant. "Shall we let Justin know?"

"Not yet. I will, afterward," he said.

"Very well: that shall be your part." Octavia was as full of repressed glee over the little secret as a child. She laid her shut fan against her lips and then touched it to his shoulder, in her haste to caution him that they should say no more, because Justin was about coming towards them. This, to be sure, was a trifle; but it would be singular if she did not perceive what influence such trifles must have upon Oliphant. At any rate, the effect was clear to others when Octavia invited Oliphant, Vivian, and Craig to dinner one evening. The younger couple made some approach to composing their quarrel, and did not stay very late; but Oliphant irresolutely hung back from going, and finally remained longer. He did not dare as yet to come to the climax of a full avowal, but they dropped into reflections more or less personal, which led very close to it.

When she was once more alone, Octavia began to wonder what was going to be the result of such trifles, upon *her*. She still felt an unreasoning resentment against Oliphant, yet her moments of relenting were becoming more frequent. Just now, as she sat by her window, trying to read, a microscopic insect — a winged life no bigger than a pin-head — fluttered in, and began executing the craziest spirals around her lamp, always dropping upon the page, on what served it as a back; whereat it went instantly into a frantic spasm, closing with a general wriggle of legs and wings that brought it upright again. There was something so irrational about this tiny creature that it acquired a likeness to humanity, which amused Octavia. She stopped reading, to watch it; but her thoughts returned to Oliphant. "Why should I care what he feels?" she mused. "He asked if I forgave him, and I said, 'You couldn't have done differently.' Well, I suppose *he* couldn't: another man might have. If he is punished, will it be my fault?" At length, noticing the insect again, she brushed it away carelessly, and ended its existence.

Whether it were the insect or Oliphant that oppressed her conscience, she slept ill that night, and woke with an unappeased questioning at her heart, still. There is, in one sense, no untruth: what seems so is merely the shadow from some cloud of personal temperament, floating between our deeper selves and the sun of truth. The shadows could not be without the light; but light does not depend for its existence on shadow. This nullity of untruth is what makes it difficult for us, when groping through the gradations of shadow in our own minds, to know just the degree of error that obscures our sight. And so Octavia was unable to make out whether she was quite veracious or not.

The general talk, however, of those who kept the run of such matters was that the affair had arrived at a point where an engagement must soon follow. Mrs. Farley Blazer let it be known that she was delighted with the romantic conjunction. Mrs. Richards said to Mary Deering that the wedding ought to come off during the Newport season; and that, as Octavia was a widow, she would probably have to be "married in a bonnet" (and, incidentally, in a church). Mrs. Deering, in reply, observed that there was the best sort of promise for happiness in the match: "Because, you know, Mrs. Gifford had such a devoted husband; and when widows have had one good husband they are generally kinder the second time — to make up for past faults and get even with their consciences. Eugene will appreciate this in Octavia, because he *didn't* have much happiness from *his* marriage."

Views of this sort having been circulated, Josephine came to Octavia and asked her, "Do you know what everybody is saying?"

"'I decline to be interviewed,'" said Octavia, parting her lips in a perverse little laugh.

"Seriously, my dear," insisted her friend, "you ought to think about it — you ought to think what you are doing."

"Well; and perhaps I have thought," Octavia retorted.

"Oh, you are in earnest, then?"

"Did I say I was?"

"No," answered Josephine. "But surely"— She finished by a fixed gaze of melancholy intentness, which made Octavia nervous. I may add that this quietude verging on sadness, characteristic of Josephine, had been growing upon her of late. Even Oliphant had made observation of it in the fleeting glimpses he had had of her when she came over to a ball, or a strolling play at the Casino Theatre; and it had resulted that she rose upon his reveries, now and then, mildly radiant and serious like the evening star.

"I'll tell you how it seems to me," she slowly recommenced, to Octavia. "Of course I didn't need other people to show me that you have been drawing him on: I've seen that for some time. But I don't think you mean to marry him."

"What right have you to say that?" exclaimed Octavia, growing fiery.

"Why, it would be inconsistent with all your principles — every thing you've ever said to me about marrying again." This was Josephine's response, and she too gave signs of a rising temperature.

"Ah, Josephine," Octavia was swift in retorting, "how can you let yourself criticise me so? Suppose I had reconsidered my principle?"

Josephine did not glide into easy acquiescence. "This is too bad," she said forlornly. "I can't believe you've changed your mind. And yet, and yet — oh, *is* it true, Octavia? You're deceiving that man!"

"I deceiving?" echoed the other woman. "What do we all do, at times? If I was sure I was very fond of him, and kept back the truth, that wouldn't be deceit, I suppose. And if I dislike him for any reason, and yet treat him well, that isn't any more deceitful. But did you ever hear what De Musset makes a character say in one of his plays? — 'Are you sure that every thing in a woman lies, when her tongue does?' Why should I tell you this: can't you guess how hard it is to know one's own mind?"

"Yes, I understand it well!" cried Josephine, starting up. The evening star had lost her pensive repose: her face was tumultuous, now, with feeling, which she tried hard to suppress. "But you have gone too far to be uncertain. It is not right: I cannot stand by and see this, much as I have loved you, Octavia. Mr. Oliphant doesn't deserve to be jilted. I came to you, hoping to persuade you; but, if that won't do, I shall look for some other way to save him. He *must* be told what you're preparing for him!"

Octavia's face lighted with a singular sort of triumph. "Then *you* love him!" she said, significantly. "Poor child, you have been so hasty that you have betrayed yourself!" Josephine turned away, blushing. "Have you told Perry Thorburn so? If you are going to warn Mr. Oliphant of any thing, how will it do for me to warn Perry?"

There was an instant of struggle, of effort on the part of Josephine to assume a silent pride; but the attempt failed, and she clutched at Octavia's hand with her own, which missed its grasp and fastened only upon a fold of the widow's dress. "Oh, you don't know," she said, in a detached, uncertain way. "You musn't think that about me. And I — won't think any thing about you, except that I hope you'll be good to him. And don't — don't speak to Perry!"

XII.

IN THE FOOTSTEPS OF FATE.

THE discovery of Josephine's hidden predilection for Oliphant brought upon Octavia a rush of new excitement which she could not fathom or control. That fine sheathing of comparative indifference, which had enabled her to go on thus far without sacrificing her peace of mind, suddenly vanished, and she ceased to be merely a spectator of her relations with Oliphant. Like an actress carried away by her part, she became subject to the situation; no longer felt that she was moulding it, but rather that she was at the mercy of events.

She was willing to confess, now, that during the busy weeks of their acquaintance a strong admiration for Oliphant had grown up in her mind. She had not suspected that a character so little salient, a presence so quiet, could acquire such sway over her; yet it had come to pass that if she missed seeing him for a single day she was conscious of a void and blankness in the day's experience. There was a silent persuasive power about him, a something calmly strong, which had caused a belief to gain upon her that his worth was sound and complete beyond that of men who might be more brilliant, or of more flexible mind. And now her belief and her admiration were confirmed by the deep impression he had made upon Josephine. Who would ever have dreamed that the self-possessed, ambitious girl could fall in love with him? For a moment, indeed, Octavia allowed herself to doubt that it could be so. "At any rate," she thought, "if she does love him, what does it amount to? Nothing but an icicle giving back a ray of the sun. She's too cold. She *can't* love him as — as *I* could." But those unspoken words brought blushes to her cheeks, and frightened her. Was it already possible for her to come to such a climax, even in fancy?

Moreover, had she not decided that love was an illusion, a tradition, a thing no one could be sure of? If this was her conviction, surely she could not pretend to any thing more than a friendly sentiment towards Oliphant; yet it irked her to suppose that she could be inferior to Josephine in the capacity for an honest and trusting affection. Besides, it was beyond all dispute that Oliphant cared for her, and not for Josephine. The knowledge gratified her; but at the next instant she was thrilled by a notion of renouncing him for herself, and making him marry Josephine. It was delightful to think how noble such a proceeding would be. Before she had time, however, to sketch it out in all its bearings, she had abandoned the scheme, and dropped helplessly back into the vortex of uncertainty from which circumstances would not permit her to escape.

Retreat might be another alternative; but what would

become of her purpose, then? Had she not made an inward vow? Was there not a duty for her to perform, a revenge to take? Anger and pity and a gathering tenderness swept by turns through her heart, confusing her more and more; but one thing, she saw, was decided: there could be no retreat. In the restlessness engendered by this conflict, she had gone out upon the grounds of High Lawn, after Josephine's visit, and was walking aimlessly among the trees, when she saw a man's figure passing up the driveway to the house. She could not tell who it was, but her heart throbbed quickly; she at once thought of Eugene. Returning by a door near the silk-panelled room, she was disappointed to find that it was Raish Porter who awaited her. But he brought an invitation that promptly enlivened the coloring of her mood; for he had devised a yachting party, to come off the next day, in which the Wares, Count Fitz-Stuart, Josephine, Oliphant, and several others would be included. Mrs. Farley Blazer was not invited, and Octavia consented with eager readiness to go.

"It's unusual to get people out on that sort of trip, here," said Raish, "and I'm as elated at my success as the sailor I've heard of, who fiddled so well that the whales all came round him to be harpooned."

Raish's jovial deportment had nothing to do with the placidity that returned to Octavia. It was the prospect of the excursion that brought back her good spirits. Her perplexities were not solved, but they had disappeared: the knowledge that she was to have Oliphant by her side, on the yacht, furnished a thread which she was content to take for her clew through the maze, at present.

It was a cool morning when Raish's small schooner-yacht, the Amaranth, glided out of the harbor, leaving behind the fossil part of Newport, with its tape-measure sidewalks and huddled gambrel-roofs, and quaint, cramped old Thames Street. The sky was half-clouded, like a face softened by pensive memories; but the gayety of the sailing-party was not abated, and their light talk and laughter around the deck played sympathetically into the murmur of the rippling tide. Smoothly the trim craft ran past Fort Adams and the bare hills arrayed in dull green, or, where the sun shone, in a warm, smiling brown that held a hint of rose; past the Point of Trees and Ramshead, too, with Conanicut on the right, all blended of mild grays and varying greens, except for its border of rough rock harsh with shadow. Then, as they made out into the open ocean, they saw a white strip of marguerites, like a broad chalk-streak, amid the green on the right, and far away a line of blue and purple heights. Under the changing heaven Beaver Tail Light, with its blanched tower on the long, low point, was brought out in white-spotted clearness by wandering sunbeams, and swiftly reduced to moist dimness again, as if it had been a lantern-picture abruptly dissolving.

"Look there!" said Raish, pointing to the cliff, as the Amaranth buffeted her way gayly across the stronger waves that met them after they had passed Gooseberry Island and Spouting Rock. "Look at that row of summer palaces! Where can you show me any thing to equal it? Think of all that growing out of the quiet little town behind it, dressed in Quaker gray and white."

"The wicked worldling," said Octavia, with a smile, "coming after the stern and pious parent."

"It's a great contrast," Oliphant assented. "I should like to know what is to be the result of the new development."

"I'll tell you," said Raish, addressing several of the group. "We have three epochs represented here: first, the early settlers, by the old stone mill; then the defunct American democracy, who built the older part of the town; and these villas here, standing for the present American oligarchy. After that will come — revolution."

He shrugged his shoulders, and looked quite French; that is, like a cynic suddenly disordered by a gust of prophecy.

"*Mais non.* How can you think possible?" Fitz-Stuart exclaimed, a diminutive consternation agitating his features.

"But, Mr. Porter," objected Vivian, "revolution belongs to the effete monarchies, you know. Surely, you don't think we can descend to borrowing any thing of the kind from them."

"Why not?" Raish answered. "We imitate them in every thing else, as far as possible; and we'll have to end by imitating them in that, too."

Josephine laughed. "*I* shall be safe, at any rate," said she. "When the time comes, and you are all blown up over here at Newport, I shall be quietly eat-ing bread and milk in Jamestown. That's the advantage of being pastoral and innocent."

As the rest broke into a general buzz of conversation, Oliphant said to her, "I shouldn't think Jamestown would be likely to satisfy *you*."

"To tell you the truth," she replied frankly, in a lower voice, "it doesn't. I'd rather be in Newport and be destroyed with the rest, if it came to that."

"Oh, Raish is talking nonsense," he said.

"I'm not so sure," Josephine answered, slowly. "We're often told that society is in an unhealthy state, and I almost believe it is."

"Then why are you so fond of it?"

"Well, it's like taking arsenic, you know. If you once begin, even in small doses, you get to depending on it. But what's your taste, Mr. Oliphant? Don't you like arsenic?"

"I'm afraid I do," he said, unconsciously stealing a glance at Octavia. "I've begun to, lately. But there was a time when I used to dream of an idyllic sort of life in some sleepy little place not too far out of the world."

"Like Jamestown?"

"Possibly."

A gentle dreaminess suffused her face. "It might be a very happy life," she said, "under certain conditions." And as her eyes met his, he thought he saw burning deep within them a peculiarly tremulous flame.

"Why isn't Perry Thorburn here to-day?" he asked, glancing around as if the young man might have been hidden in the cabin and were about to emerge.

"I'm sure I don't know," said Josephine. "Does his absence trouble you?"

He saw that she was annoyed by his question, which was a too significant one. Accordingly he began to praise the absent Perry, telling her that he had grown to like him very much. "Still," he added, smiling in a gallant manner, "I can get along perfectly without him, at present."

This speech was not a success, either. It was a refinement of pain to poor Josephine, who knew how superficial the complimentary tone must be, since his heart was really with Octavia. But she concealed its effect upon her, and kept him engaged in talk, drawing him always a little deeper, and always with that strange trembling light in her eyes. Oliphant felt the fascination, and even felt that he might begin to succumb to it before long. Meanwhile Octavia was left mainly to the attentions of Stillman Ware, who remarked with great satisfaction that Fitz-Stuart was progressing admirably with Vivian: they had gone away by themselves towards the forward part of the yacht, under the shadow of the foresail, and were apparently engrossed with each other. Oliphant several times resolved to move away from Josephine, but he still remained by her. She knew the power of the spell she could exercise, and had recklessly resolved to use it. Was it not her right, by nature? Moreover, if Octavia was bent upon trifling with this man, any means were justifiable for saving him, even to winning him away from her. And Oliphant, though he did not know her motive, became conscious that she exhibited a singular interest in him. Shall we admit that the discovery excited his vanity? Or shall we say that he enjoyed it because it was extraneous evidence, giving him a sense of his value, which made it seem less audacious for him to hope that he could gain Octavia's love?

Octavia watched them, at first with scorn for what she considered Josephine's unfairness, and then with a rankling envy of her friend's easy power: finally, the desire to bring Oliphant to her feet — whether for mere triumph, or for the securing of a genuine happiness, she scarcely knew — began to rise to the point of fever.

The situation was broken by an announcement of lunch in the cabin, made by Raish's negro steward, Fortune.

"Isn't he a perfect specimen?" Porter asked his guests, as they assembled to go in. "You noticed the wonderful curl of his hair, I suppose. Why, it's so woolly that positively he has to put camphor in it, early in the summer, to keep the moths out!"

Porter, as usual when at table, was in the best of spirits, and soon allayed the conflict and agitation that were threatened in the minds of Octavia, Oliphant, and Josephine. Several dainty and elaborate courses were served, but the choicest dish of all consisted of broiled green plover served on plates which had been washed in champagne. "It's the only way to get the finest flavor," Raish declared; "and the only thing I know of that comes anywhere near plover served like this is the 'larks stewed in morning's roseate breath, or roasted by a sunbeam's splendor,' which Tom Moore once offered to the Marquis of Lansdowne."

He was so gay that one would have thought he hadn't a care in the world; but as a matter of fact he had not at all enjoyed Josephine's proceedings toward Oliphant, since it was for his own interest that Perry's attachment for her should come to a prosperous issue. He was disappointed, too, at Perry's failure to join the party, and still more disturbed by the knowledge that that young speculator had not yet actually taken or paid for the Orbicular stock which he proposed to buy. But, as I say, he kept his company in capital humor. They suspected nothing; and if he had never been going to give another entertainment — if he and they had all been destined to fade away into the mists and be seen no more, with the Amaranth turning to a phantom yacht under their feet — he could not have made a happier ending.

But they had no intention of fading. When they came out, with smiling lips and with the delicate tingle of wine in their veins, the mists had disappeared, and they turned to make the run homeward in a soft glow of sunshine. As they approached within a certain distance of the shore, a strange phenomenon saluted them. All at once the saltness of the air seemed to cease; the wind came from off the land, and poured around them in a breath of honey the mingled scent of flowers by thousands in the rich villa-gardens of Newport, and in the fields far away. It was an intoxicating aroma; it was like the exhalation from some enchanted territory of delights. In a minute or so, with a veering of the wind, it had passed; but Oliphant, hanging over Octavia, murmured, "This is a good omen for our return to land, isn't it?"

"Yes; a much more hopeful one than the chilly mist we sailed out with."

And there was a new significance in her gaze, as she spoke with lifted face, — a significance that referred to his lingering near Josephine so long before lunch, and to the slight shadow of jealousy which she allowed to rest upon her own mind, and was willing that he should perceive.

He sat down beside her, his face radiant with something more than the sunshine, and remained there until they came into port. He had made another advance; they had entered a new phase in their friendship; and to him the understanding established between them was the next thing to a mutual confession. Still, when he landed, he felt that he had left behind him, on that little voyage, the last vestige of the independence which had been his at the beginning of the season; and this independence, albeit one of loneliness and sorrow, was something the loss of which might have to be regretted. He was drifting, now; he was at her mercy he knew; yet the fact was sweet to him, and he rejoiced in it. One must "give all for love;" but the price was not too great.

He longed to put his fate to the test; but somehow there was difficulty in finding room for any action so momentous in the crowded round of social occupations. The very next day was to culminate in that brilliant musical drainage entertainment, the well-vouched-for benefit concert in aid of Dana Sweetser's movement, at which Justin was to make his public *début;* and during most of the interval Oliphant was busy in assisting about the final arrangements.

With the social support which had been pledged to it, the concert could not have missed being the success it was. Mrs. Farley Blazer would have done all the injury she could to the enterprise, because of Justin's participation, except for the restraint put upon her by friendly regard for Dana. This prevented her active hostility, and she compromised by sending Tilly and Lord Hawkstane, in charge of some friends, while she herself staid at home. Mrs. Chauncey Ware, however, threw her patronage unreservedly into the scales on Dana's side; and the sibylline scrolls of gray hair that identified as hers a certain black bonnet, from under which they projected, were seen in one row of chairs with Stillman and Vivian and Count Fitz-Stuart. The mother and brother were thus gracious in respect of Justin because they believed the coolness that obviously had interposed between him and Vivian was to be permanent; and in the fulness of their gratitude to Providence for the sacred gift of this lovers' quarrel, they were able to spare a little generosity for the young musician.

I am not going to describe the concert, but from the interest which Vivian Ware took in the music it must have been passably good. Several times she bent her head and wrote comments on the programme, with the small gold pencil which the count lent her for the purpose, and then folded up the paper, as if the brief record of her pleasure were too precious to be exposed to the outer air. The count betrayed a lover-like curiosity to see what she had written, but with corresponding coquetry she kept putting him off, and he did not get a sight of it, the whole evening.

After the performance, Justin appeared for two or three minutes in the eddying drift of copious silks, light shoulder-wraps, and black coats, moving towards the exit. Octavia in her pansy bonnet and Oliphant in evening dress were there to welcome him with hearty praise; many by-standers regarded him with manifest admiration; and as he drew near Vivian, she was so eager to thank him for his playing, that she dropped her programme in turning to meet him. He caught it before it had reached the floor, and offered to return it to her.

"Never mind," she said. "It has some notes of my impressions. Keep it, and tell me by and by if I am right."

Justin bowed, and almost instantly glided away. The count at first looked mortified that the programme should have escaped him; but the expression was followed by one of serenity, as of a man who could afford so trifling a loss, in view of what he retained; and so he went out with Vivian to join Stillman, who was busy finding the carriage.

XIII.

HAWKS AND DOVES.

THE episode of the programme, however, had not escaped the notice of one or two ladies who were standing near.

They belonged to a small coterie which was in the habit of meeting every day or two at the houses of the several acquaintances who composed it. The members of this circle gathered together for self-improvement; that is, they devoted an hour to trimming and polishing their finger-nails, by means of the latest and most improved apparatus. This species of culture induced in them a liberality which extended to the improvement of other people, so far as that could be done by defining and thoroughly discussing their demerits, in order that if those persons *should* improve every one would know exactly how much they had done so.

Pious Mrs. Ballard Mole was one of this group. It had been proposed by somebody to hold concerts at the Casino on Sunday evenings, and this was enough to deter Mrs. Ballard Mole from going to any musical affair in that place, however worthy the object. None the less, though, was she willing to listen to reports of what had occurred at the Sweetser entertainment; and when Miss De Peyster (Roland's ugly sister) began to say something about the strangeness of Vivian's remark to Craig, Mrs. Mole experienced a chilly joy in thinking that if any germ of scandal had effected a lodgment in that distinguished audience, it was only a righteous judgment on the projectors of chimerical Sunday concerts that had not come to pass. .

"There seems to be something between those two,— some understanding that isn't quite right, under the circumstances," said Miss De Peyster, opening her case of nail instruments, and inspecting them as if she had been a surgeon about to begin vivisection.

She was seated on the broad veranda, shaded by vines and canvas curtains, of Mrs. Mole's scriptural villa, called Petra, on the Cliff, where the conclave had been called for that morning.

"Then, do you consider Vivian engaged to the count?" asked Mary Deering, who was one of the worldly representatives in this little circle.

"Well, if she isn't, it's about time she should be," Miss De Peyster answered, clicking her scissors sharply.

"Oh, do you know what I heard yesterday?" This question proceeded from a lady who wore a jaunty ruby-tinted turban, and enjoyed great intimacy with Mrs. Farley Blazer.

"No; what?" "Any thing about the count?" Uttering responses of this sort, everybody became attentive, and there was a momentary pause in the wielding of their small steel weapons.

"Yes; the count. Dana Sweetser says he was

walking, the other morning, over where the Cliff begins, you know, — that bare spot where it's so quiet, — and he noticed three Frenchmen sitting on the grass, with a basket of breakfast and some claret; and they were talking quite loud and laughing, don't you know, so they didn't notice him. And he made out that they were creditors of the count's. They're lying in wait for him, in a sort of way; at any rate, watching him. Mr. Sweetser says he believes they even have a detective keeping his eye on Hartman's, where the count stays, you know. Isn't it odd, — a man who might have been King of England, may be, having creditors after him?"

The rest agreed that it was *very* odd, and that the count's speedy engagement to Vivian, with a claim on the Ware property, ought to be wished for by every one who understood the pathos of the situation.

"Besides," Mrs. Mole declared, "he's a much more desirable person than that penniless pianist."

"But Mr. Craig plays the organ in church," Mary Deering suggested, with a spice of malice, and spoiled the effect of her shot by sending off another: "The count is penniless, too, it appears."

"Temporarily, my dear," Mrs. Ballard Mole retorted, assuming a mien of devout loyalty. "Temporarily penniless; that is all. It can't last."

"The creditors evidently think it can't, or sha'n't," whispered Mary to Mrs. Richards, who was present.

Then they all began talking about other things and people. There were rumors of an approaching divorce, to be assorted; and the ladies next devoted themselves sadly to comment on various unfortunate traits in their associates, which ought to be corrected, as well as to the ins and outs of sundry quarrels that had begun to shatter the harmony of Newport society. Gradually an approach was made to the subject of Mrs. Blazer's confidential relations with Porter; though, in deference to Mrs. Blazer's friend, who was there, the approach was characterized by Christian tenderness.

"It's really a pity, you know," said Miss De Peyster to the friend, "when her husband is about, and they're not living together. *I* don't believe there's any thing in it, you know; but so many *will* take that view."

Mrs. Richards burst into uncontrollable laughter. "Oh, the funniest thing yet!" she ejaculated, while the jewels on her generous bosom shook with sympathetic humor. "Sarah Loyall made a mistake yesterday, and called Mr. Porter 'Mr. Blazer,' in Mrs. Blazer's presence. But she was equal to the occasion: she said, 'Oh, Mrs. Loyall, don't make him out to be any thing so disagreeable as a husband!' Wasn't that rich?"

There was great amusement on the veranda, at this; even the ruby-turbaned friend of Mrs. Blazer joining in the merriment.

Snip, snip, went the scissors, as the ladies chattered on, and deftly labored to modify the lingering vestiges of a savage state at the termination of their soft, white fingers. The scissors were stumpy, curved and sharply pointed like the beaks of hawks; and as they continued their work they seemed at the same time to be tearing numerous reputations into fragments.

Mrs. Deering finished her task first, and, being obliged to go, bade the rest good-morning. As soon as she had disappeared, the lady in the ruby turban saw an opportunity to equalize matters for Mrs. Farley Blazer by introducing a slight diversion at Mary's expense.

"I'm afraid," she observed, "our last remarks weren't entirely agreeable to Mrs. Deering."

"Oh," began Mrs. Ballard Mole, "on account of"—

"Mr. Atlee, of course," supplemented Mrs. Richards.

"It really is becoming disgraceful," said the ruby turban, "the way those two are going on. It grows worse and worse."

"Can't something be done to stop it?" queried Mrs. Mole, in a regenerating frame of mind. "I really wish there could."

"Stop it?" Miss De Peyster shrilled. "Stop an avalanche! Why, he goes with her everywhere,— driving, hunting. polo; and not satisfied with that, they take quiet walks together in the twilight. Then they are on the Cliff, Sundays. He never goes to church with her, I notice. but he spends a great deal of time at the house, and is constantly there at dinner while Mr. Deering is in New York. I should think she would have some consideration for her children's sakes, at least. What she can find in the man, either! Really and truly, I think *some*times people ought just to be exiled!"

An instant's silence intervened after this outburst;

and then Mrs. Richards said sweetly, "My dear, you shouldn't use the steel. It's injurious." She referred merely to the fact that Miss De Peyster, in her preoccupied excitement, was rather fiercely prodding one of her finger-nails with the smooth end of a flat steel file.

They had now reached the powdering and polishing stage of their work, and the remarks interchanged gradually took on a more suave and dignified character.

The reflections which had been made upon Mary Deering were not, however, confined to the self-improving coterie whose confidences we have allowed ourselves to summarize. Oliphant had here and there come upon the traces of similar ones, which, aided by his own observation, had disturbed him excessively. He noticed the increasing imprudence of his cousin's conduct; also that Roger now came on to Newport less frequently than before, and that when he did come there was a queer kind of restraint on his part towards his wife. The ruddy-faced, short-haired broker's former air of confidence was perceptibly subdued. To Oliphant the change was pathetic, and he had resolved to speak to his cousin seriously. He fancied that he understood the case. Mary Deering had simply had her head turned by the frivolities of the place, and had been led into making an idol of this Anglicized nonentity, who to her mind represented the most important local tendency. Nevertheless, she ought not to carry her idolatry too far.

Obeying his advisory impulse, he betook himself to her house, on the second day after the concert; but

Mary was not at home. He decided to wait; and in a moment or two, seeing the door into the dining-room half open and some one apparently seated at the table there, he moved to the threshold, half believing that it was Atlee. With a rush of sudden anger, he determined to upbraid the dandy, and so stepped forward vigorously. But, to his astonishment, he beheld only little Clarence in a chair by the table.

The boy had a glass of claret and water before him, and was smoking a cigarette.

"What does this mean?" cried Oliphant. "Are you crazy, Clarence?"

"I'm trying to soothe my nerves," the child answered, looking up wearily at him. Oliphant was horrified at the premature age in his unformed little countenance. He stood speechless. "It's just what papa does now," Clarence continued, calmly, "whenever he comes here. I don't know what the matter is, but"— At this point he slid from his chair, and rapidly made his way towards Oliphant. "Oh, cousin Oliphant, papa doesn't seem a bit happy! Last time he came here, he took me out on the piazza, and mamma and Mr. Atlee were talking all the time, inside here, and papa said to me, he asked me,—wasn't it queer? — if I didn't want to go away with him back to New York, or way out West somewhere; and I said I didn't, unless mamma and all of us were going. And then he said, 'Um,' like that,"— Clarence pursed his lips up severely,—"and he said he didn't think there was any room for us here, he did. Now what did he mean, cousin Oliphant?"

His cousin took him by the hand and led him away into the other room, sickened and aghast by the dreary, unconscious revelation; but just as he was making a suitably superficial reply, Mary Deering appeared from the hall.

She dismissed Clarence with harsh peremptoriness, to his nurse, and returned to Oliphant, looking, as he conceived, rather distraught and ill at ease. It was late; the dusk was beginning to throw its soft folds of crape around the trees and the house, casting deeper shadows into the small interior. Oliphant thought Mrs. Deering must have a prescient sense of his object in calling upon her. Ah, how sadly unlike that bright, playfully mischievous face with which she met him when he first dropped down in Newport was the mobile, anxious one that he saw opposite to him now!

A crisis impended. He opened his attack weakly with some general inquiries about Roger.

Suddenly they heard steps ascending to the piazza. There was an impetuous knock at the door. Again Oliphant thought of Atlee, and became so excited that he braced himself for a personal encounter. Mary Deering, overwrought and expectant of some painful scene, uttered a low cry. But, as they rose to meet the new-comer, their suspense relaxed; for it was Stillman Ware whom they descried in the increasing gloom.

"Is my sister here?" he inquired at once.

They both answered, "No."

"I meant," said Stillman, in a shaky and unnerved sort of way, "is Mr. Oliphant here? Ah, yes, that is Mr. Oliphant. I have just been to Mrs. Gifford's to look for my sister; and she isn't there. We can't find her. Do you know any thing about young Craig's movements?"

"Nothing," returned Oliphant, "except that he told me he should be out of town this afternoon."

"Then," cried Stillman, clapping one hand to his distracted little bald forehead, "they have gone together! My God, Oliphant, she has run away with him!"

XIV.

THE FLIGHT OF A METEOR.

NO one could tell how the elopement had come about, but every one was voluble in relating that the event had really taken place, and there were many wild rumors and surmises added to the fact. It was said that several persons had suspected that something of the kind was about to happen; there was also a story of a clandestine meeting effected by the two young people near the Forty Steps, the night after the concert. A servant had seen a woman's white figure in the grassy street there, which was presently joined by a dark, shadowy man, and both had disappeared over the edge of the Cliff, so that the servant had thought them to be ghosts, and kept silence, through fear. The fashionable world was excitedly scandalized; poor little Stillman continued in great agitation; Mrs. Ware took it upon herself to be "prostrated," and her course in so doing was generally approved by her friends. A search was begun for the fugitives, and Stillman even engaged detective assistance.

But, whatever else might be in doubt, it was soon made clear that Octavia and Oliphant received a large share of blame for the occurrence. The circumstance of the two runaways having dined at High Lawn with the widow and widower, a few days before, came to light, and was construed as a proof of connivance. It was also remembered that, on the previous Sunday, Octavia and Oliphant had strolled on the Cliff Walk with Justin, and that, by turning often, they kept meeting Vivian, who was likewise sauntering in the throng there with Count Fitz-Stuart.

In reality our friends knew nothing about the scheme; but the false construction placed upon them was strengthened by Oliphant's receiving very promptly a message from Craig, dated at Tiverton, and saying that Vivian and he, having been quietly married, had taken lodging for a short time in that modest and drowsy watering-place, which gazes so meekly from the mainland towards the prouder shores of Aquidneck Island. The reason for their precipitancy was that the count, becoming urgent, and being sustained by Mrs. Chauncey Ware and Stillman, had insisted upon an ultimate decision as to his suit, and Vivian had been driven to an unexpected mode of settling the question.

Oliphant hastened by the first train to Tiverton; and finding that Justin had no capital beyond two or three hundred dollars, a large part of which he had received for his services in the Sweetser concert, he made the heartiest offers of assistance. "You know," he said, "I was going to send you to Germany. I meant to hand you, as a first instalment, a thousand dollars. Why not take it now?"

"Because I'm not going to Germany just yet," said

Justin, with buoyant good fellowship and enviable serenity. "I shall go on with my work at Trinity and find people to take piano lessons."

"But if you need me you will let me know?," queried Oliphant almost plaintively, pleading with the portentous self-reliance of the new husband. "Miss Vivian, — Mrs. Craig, I mean, — I rely upon you to see to this;" and he appealed to her.

Vivian was dressed in white, as usual. Her costume was an expensive work of artifice, imported from Paris, which by a rare purity of outline, with a draping of folds from one shoulder across the waist, produced a semi-statuesque Greek effect, gaining piquancy from its utter inappropriateness to Vivian's quick, whimsical, and wholly modern attitudes and gestures. The three were standing on a plot of grass in front of the absurdly stunted and riotously ugly French-roofed cottage where the lovers had ensconced themselves. Vivian gave a little half jump, which disarranged her classic folds, and said, "You are a dear good fellow, Mr. Oliphant; and we appreciate you. But I'm sure my husband can make his own way. Can't you, Justin?"

She placed one hand for an instant on Justin's arm, in token of dependence and of possession, but quickly took it away again. Then she fronted towards Oliphant, with a shining happiness in her eyes, the like of which he had never seen.

He had come to play the part of a venerable benefactor, bestowing something of practical value on these children. He went away as the recipient of an inspiration from that spectacle of ideal love which made him poor by contrast, and reproached him with his poverty.

Intending to go and describe his visit to Octavia (to whom he had already sent a note saying that he had heard from the truants), he was prevented from doing so, on his return, by an occurrence so extraordinary as to merit recital.

Transcontinental Telegraph stock, under the impulse imparted to it through the private wire from Thorburn's villa, had been executing some interesting but not unnatural manœuvres. First it fell off a very little in price; then it began to rise; and as it ascended there were many purchases made on the strength of a rumor that Thorburn had gone to work in earnest to "peg" the stock quite up to par. The buyers were very confident; they wore a joyous look, as of men at last released from all harassing doubts, and kindly presented with a free pass to fortune. No one could explain precisely why the thing was so certain, but few thought of questioning. It was one of those grand spontaneous movements of the human mind which, in Wall Street, teach us that faith in the unseen and the unknowable still survives, however much the churches may bemoan its decline. Suddenly, however, Transcontinental began to go down again. It dropped below the point from which it had started, and kept on sinking, by eighths and quarters, from one figure to another, with ominous regularity. Did this shake the sublime confidence of the multitude? Not at all. A few timid souls here and there shrank affrighted, and parted with their holdings; but there were plenty of people who had bought at the highest prices, and now not only kept increasing their margins, but also invested in more shares.

Their courage was apparently justified when the stock began to rally and went up several points in a few days. Many now sold out and cleared handsome amounts. Those, however, who were anxious to "get in" and go on with the flood-tide were more numerous; and Thorburn accommodated them with a good deal of stock which he had acquired at a lower price. At last, after one or two more of these ups and downs, and when Thorburn had sold a sufficient quantity "short," Transcontinental took its final plunge. It had been like a kite sailing aloft and gleefully watched by school-boys, as it rose or fell with the wind; but the pulling of the string had brought it to such a point that, without warning, the kite came tilting over on its head, and made straight for the ground.

Perry ran to his father for advice. That heroic old gentleman told him that without pluck and endurance he never would make an "operator." He pointed out some of the reasons why Transcontinental never could remain for a great length of time at the bottom of the heap.

"Still," he said, "*I* can't advise you. You must decide every thing for yourself, and make up your mind whether you are carrying too much load or not."

Re-assured, Perry held on, and many of his friends and their acquaintance, knowing this, did likewise.

Some actually continued to buy in afresh. Presently, however, he and they awoke to the fact that they were in a financial Bay of Fundy, where the ebb of the tide was abnormal and beyond their calculations. The sinking went on immitigably. Old Thorburn professed to be unable to account for it, and seemed perplexed. Then Perry, who had assumed altogether too large a risk, and was already severely depleted by his margins, decided to take care of himself. He got rid of nearly all his Transcontinental at an enormous sacrifice, paid in full for a couple of hundred shares which he retained, and found that his losses amounted to nearly fifty thousand dollars.

"Now, sir," he said to his father, with pardonable indignation in his tone, "I've acted without consulting you," and he explained his situation, omitting to speak of the shares he had kept; "but I should like to know what you meant by getting me into this trap. I consider that I've been treated outrageously!"

Old Thorburn displayed no anger. On the contrary he leaned back in his chair, beneath the spider-web design of his alcove, and laughed slyly, then broadly; finishing up with a second sly chuckle. "Why, my dear boy," said he, in his heavy, spongy voice, "what are you talking about? Can't you see the point?"

"The point, eh? Is it a joke?"

"Of course it is, — for you and me. Some of the outsiders, I suppose, think it's pretty serious. I just wanted to show you how to do things."

"Well, you've shown me how to lose fifty thousand dollars."

Old Thorburn broke into a roar of laughter. "Exactly!" he cried. "And now that you know how, don't you do it again. That's *my* advice, Perry. By George, this is the neatest piece of tactics I ever carried through!"

"You call it neat, then, to swindle your own son?" Perry inquired, with intense disgust.

"'Swindle' is your word, not mine," returned his father. "Call it what you like. *I* call it keeping my own counsel. I've taught you not to trust anybody in business,—not even me." Thorburn's manner conveyed a sort of virtuous surprise at himself that he could not be trusted. "And at the same time, I've used you to good purpose in making the mob do just what I wanted. Damn it, Perry,"—the old gentleman was beginning to exhibit heat,—"I should think you would have some kind of appreciation, instead of growling like a hurt child."

Perry's expression was far from conveying respect. "Perhaps I have *some* kind of appreciation," he said, curtly. "And now I suppose you're going to work to drive the stock up, after buying all you wanted from me and from the rest at a ruinous rate."

"We shall see," answered the elder man, crafty glee re-appearing in his eyes. "I don't like to tell you any thing about it, because you see — ha, ha! — you might not believe me."

At this climax, his merriment entirely overcame him, and Perry scornfully left him to enjoy it by himself. The only satisfaction he had was in the thought of the shares he owned, which would receive the benefit of his father's next move, and probably bring him back in the long run a third of what he had lost. Yet even this prospect gave him a certain horror of himself, because it reminded him that he was acting on the same instinct of deceit which struck him as so hideous in his father.

Thorburn senior proceeded to encourage the market, for the purpose of realizing the immense profits which formed the object of all his strategy; but his victims were, for the most part, too much crippled to take the field again and share in the benefit of the gradual rise which presently began. Many of them, indeed, were wrecked for life by the terrible throw their invisible antagonist had given them.

Raish Porter was a heavy sufferer; and, besides being greatly out of pocket, he had to endure the disappointment of learning that Perry, owing to the absorption of half his private property in the recent "deal," would be unable to take at present the block of Orbicular stock which had been promised him. It was a painful crisis for Raish; but he did not lose his nerve. His quiet, searching eye remained imperturbable as ever; his bluff, self-confident demeanor underwent no change; and perhaps he would have found a way out of his dilemma, had it not been for sundry other unlucky accidents.

Mr. Hobart had become dissatisfied with the slow progress of the Orbicular Company, from which as yet he could get no return on his investment; and, what was more serious, he began to evince suspicion regarding the value of the company's patents. Raish suggested that he should ask Judge Malachi Hixon to confer with his (Raish's) lawyer, Strange, and investigate the subject anew. Raish was fond of extolling the judge's incorruptibility, but this was chiefly with a feeling that it might some time be peculiarly useful to have Hixon considered unimpeachable; privately, he believed that he could insinuate his own prepared statements into that gentleman's mind, and induce him to ratify them.

Accordingly it was settled that Strange should call upon the judge, at the Ocean House. He did so, and was courteously received by the learned Malachi, who was grappling at the moment with an especially huge and black cigar, the pressure of his lips upon which greatly increased the usual complexity of wrinkles in his face.

"So you think this is a good thing, Mr. Strange?" he asked.

"Oh, excelsior," said Strange, casually as it were, and softly. He was a small, dexterous, accommodating man, with a conical head, which looked as if it would make a great effort to pass through almost any required knot-hole.

"Have you got any papers with you — schedules, lists of the patents, and so forth?"

"Why, certainly; any amount," Mr. Strange replied, apparently eager to empty the contents of his satchel. But, after bustling at it, he paused, and launched into a general disquisition. He told of the marvellous growth of the corporation, and named some of the substantial men who held its stock; and he was very ingenuous and pleasing and enthusiastic, altogether.

Judge Hixon, nevertheless, continued to mention the papers. Strange showed him one or two, and then, after feeling around a little, came to his point. "I've told you enough in a general way," he said, "to satisfy you of the excellence of the concern and its prospects. We should like very much to have you for a stockholder, judge, — very much, indeed. Now, any thing you can do in the way of satisfying Mr. Hobart, or any one else who should fall into similar confusion about the details of the affair, will be of as much service to my client, of course, as to Mr. Hobart. Mr. Porter can let you have five thousand dollars' worth of the stock, just as well as not, and — and you needn't pay for it until convenient."

Mr. Strange was bland, but slightly nervous: his conical head was, figuratively, preparing to dodge. Judge Malachi Hixon straightened up in his chair, and removed his right leg from its resting-place on the knee of the left. He gazed steadily at Mr. Strange, who hastily noted the judge's resemblance to a harassed and dejected specimen of the American eagle, and was in suspense as to which of the attributes of that typical bird the judge was about to offer, — the arrows or the olive-branch.

"It is a very liberal proposition," said Judge Hixon slowly. "I haven't got any too much money laid up, and this may prove profitable. Did you bring the stock with you?"

"Oh, yes," said Strange, diving into his bag with the greatest alacrity.

"Never mind it now," resumed the judge, genially, taking the cigar out of his mouth and letting the wrinkles ameliorate themselves. Then he placed it between his teeth once more, and the wrinkles all came back. "You can wait till I send for it," he explained. "Meanwhile, leave me any papers you like, and I will look them over."

"With the greatest pleasure," said Strange, and left a few.

He reported his success to Raish. The game had always worked well before, and they had no reason to suppose that it would not do so now. But Malachi Hixon immediately set to work investigating in earnest. He started the district attorney in New York upon the case, and rapidly pumped into his own mental reservoir whatever knowledge Hobart had of the company's transactions. By means of brief research and some detective work, it was found that the enterprise had been built up from small beginnings by advertising in metropolitan journals, then copying these advertisements with laudatory notices in rural papers throughout several States, and by sustaining a showy office upon the receipts which rapidly flowed in. Apparently, all the money obtained was spent in clerk-hire and more advertising. Then Porter had flown for higher game; and, through his business and social connections, had induced a number of capitalists to put in considerable sums. The district attorney was surprised at some of the names Strange had given him, but his inquiry corroborated the list. Little by little, he ascertained that these men were convinced that the

Orbicular Manufacturing Company was fraudulent, but did not dare to appear against its promoter, for fear of injuring their own credit with the banks; since a prosecution must reveal their want of judgment in making such an investment. Fortunately Hobart, being a man of irritable leisure, and vindictive as well, was not restrained by any such scruples.

It was important, however, to obtain further evidence of imposture by proving the unauthorized character of some of the manufactures contemplated by Raish. Unexpectedly, this came to hand, through the labors of the detective. A workman employed in another machine-shop was brought to confess that he had traced the patterns of appliances made by his employers, and had furnished them to Raish, who in turn had had drawings made from them, with which he shrewdly dazzled the minds of successive investors.

On the evening of Oliphant's return from Tiverton, after he had dined comfortably at the Queen Anne cottage with Raish, the latter noticed that his guest was thoughtful and looked despondent. The truth is, Eugene was overburdened with anxiety for the results of Justin's rash proceeding, with worry about Mary Deering, and with his own problem in connection with Octavia.

"Do you ever feel gloomy?" Raish asked him, blowing out a cloud of smoke which thinly veiled the cheery twinkle of his eyes.

"Yes, I do," answered Oliphant solemnly.

"Well, *I* don't!" Raish affirmed, with hearty satisfaction. "It doesn't pay. I've seen a good many vicissitudes, and I've been through more than one Saturday night when I didn't have a red cent in my pocket, and didn't know where my Sunday's dinner was coming from. But I've always smoked the best cigars and drank the very best wines, and I never have felt gloomy."

There was such a superabundance of ease and buoyancy in Raish's tone, that Oliphant began to feel decidedly better.

Ten minutes later, some one rang at the door. James returned to the parlor and announced a strange gentleman, on business. "Well, let's see him," said Raish, good-humoredly. "I haven't any appointment at this hour, but show him right in, James."

The visitor proved to be a sergeant of police, in plain clothes, with requisition papers from the Governor of Rhode Island and a warrant for Raish's arrest on a charge of obtaining money under false pretences

"Never heard any thing so ridiculous in my life!" exclaimed Raish, cordially. "How do you explain it, sergeant? Who's the complainant? By the way, have a cigar?"

"Thank you, sir," said the sergeant, accepting the favor. "The complaint was entered by Mr. Hobart. You know him, I suppose."

"I have an idea that I do," Raish responded. "But I never was aware that the Hobart I know could be so silly and suicidal as to do this. Sit down, and let's see if we can't straighten the thing out, somehow."

After a brief colloc u , Raish perceived that there

was no escape: he was given a letter from Hobart, informing him of the workman's confession. Nevertheless, he maintained his jauntiness, and proposed to the sergeant that he be allowed to remain in the house over night, and proceed to New York in the morning.

This the sergeant at first refused: he had two other officers waiting outside, and said it was impossible to keep them up all night. But Raish insisted on their being asked in. "We'll give 'em some supper, at any rate," he declared, with as much welcome as if they had been the most desired of companions. "Better stay over, sergeant," he continued, invitingly. "I'll give you all a fine sail on my yacht to Wickford, first thing in the morning, and we can take any train you like for Providence. It's nothing but a dyspeptic whim of old Hobart's," he added to Oliphant: "I don't see why I should be so inconvenienced by it."

The officer was really charmed by Raish's ease and hospitality, and at length fell in with the plan. His prisoner then applied himself to packing a valise, and setting his affairs in order as well as he could, though he was not allowed to handle a single object without close surveillance, nor to be for a moment out of sight. About one o'clock, Raish asked permission to walk up and down the open piazza at one side of the house, with Oliphant. This was granted, but the sergeant took a chair out, too, and remained on guard.

Raish tramped leisurely to and fro with his friend, talking in his customary entertaining way. All at once, Oliphant was startled out of the mood of a quiet listener by seeing Raish put his fingers into his vest-pocket and then suddenly raise his arm, carrying a small object to his lips.

Without having time to reflect, Oliphant instinctively struck down the arm and clutched Raish's hand. There was a small phial in it, which Raish attempted to throw away; but his friend was too quick for him, and seized it. The sergeant came promptly to their side, and pinioned the brilliant financier.

"Yes, it's poison," Raish confessed in a species of gasp, answering Oliphant's look of amazement and reproach. "Cyanide of potassium. In two minutes I should have been a dead man. Oh, yes, it's all up, Oliphant, my boy. Too bad, too bad!" He lifted his forehead, and gazed at the sky for an instant. "You remember what I said this evening about the best cigars?" he went on, smiling sarcastically. "Well, there they are: all those stars! Those are the smouldering stumps, it strikes me." He groaned slightly. "Ah," he cried, "I was too respectable! I ought to have been like the gamblers over there, who are plying their game at this moment, and are left in peace; or else like old Thorburn, who cleaned me out, and prevented me from warding off this accident. I'll tell you what I'm reminded of: that fellow who was porter (see the pun?) on a drawing-room car, and had a wife at each end of the line. By his painstaking diligence in bigamy he attained to the ripe honors of a term in the penitentiary; but the only thing he regretted was that he couldn't divide his term, as he had all his other possessions, between the two wives! I would be willing to make that sacrifice myself, for Thorburn and the other gamblers."

Something of his wonted hilarity returned to him as he finished. "I'm more sorry than I can tell you, for all this," said Oliphant. "Is there any thing I can do for you, Porter?"

"Nothing whatever, my boy." The sergeant here explained that he felt obliged to put handcuffs upon his prisoner, and Raish, having submitted to that operation, talked on without embarrassment. "I only want you," he said, "to recognize the correctness of what I have said to you about the hollowness and humbug of society here. I'm a humbug, and therefore I was able to perceive it all. I don't speak from envy: what good would that do me now? No, I merely notice that I am a straw on the current, or a falling cigar-stump in the sky, that shows what may happen as soon as a general overturn begins."

When the first chill and distant gray light of morning came, Oliphant accompanied his quondam host and the police officers to the wharves, whence they were rowed out to the Amaranth. He watched her getting under sail, and waited until the pretty schooner was well out in the harbor. Far above her, one star glimmered wearily in the pale, whitish-blue of the sky; but that, too, faded while the yacht was growing smaller, and disappeared.

XV.

A MAN'S ORDEAL.

THE season was now at its height. The President was in town, alternately making brief public appearances, and being spirited from house to house among the select few who had captured him, in a furtive and costly seclusion, as if he had been some influential malefactor whom it was desirable to keep out of the way. The fragments of a religious convention and those of a political reform convention, which had recently been held there, were still drifting about the place. Entertainments of the most brilliant sort were multiplied to distraction; the lawn-tennis tournament was on the point of collecting upon the Casino lawn a dense parterre of beautiful women in ravishing costumes; and in fine, the whirl of gay life, which was doomed to cease in two or three weeks more, made one think of a giant soap-bubble circling faster and faster, and gathering a wilder glow of color as the instant of bursting draws nearer.

The collapse of one adventurer like Raish Porter was a mere incident in the general history of the season's bubble; but it created a widespread and intense astonishment, and, coming so soon after the runaway marriage, it swallowed up the excitement wh.ch had eddied for a little while around Justin and Vivian.

People were greatly surprised that Raish should have turned out as he had done. And it is noticeable that this matter of how individuals "turn out" is always a great mystery to the world. The reason is that the world occupies itself with exteriors, not interiors, of character; consequently, when that which is in a man comes in due time to the front, the crowd is puzzled because he has "turned out" to public view what it might all along have known was there, had it taken the trouble to inquire within.

Mrs. Farley-Blazer was a loser to a considerable extent by the downfall of her confidential friend, companion, and adviser. She was greatly incensed at his fiasco, and the rumor soon came into circulation that she had used very profane language — as was her wont on occasions of great excitement — when news of the arrest first reached her. The financial injury done to her, although not serious in proportion to the large income allowed her by her neglected and broken-down husband, was especially exasperating because she was always averse to parting with money in any way, and because she had made up her mind, immediately on Vivian's elopement, to purchase Count Fitz-Stuart for her niece Ruth, by paying off his debts. That expense, which had already caused her much anticipatory anguish, yet was inevitable, now became a source of redoubled pain.

But it was Oliphant who, though not entangled in the wreck, felt its immediate effects in the most tangible way. Raish's property was all promptly attached, including the yacht, his horses and equipages, and whatever belonged to him in the Craig cottage. The household came, as a matter of course, to a dead stop, and the servants prepared to leave. Oliphant, however, had an inspiration: he saw an opportunity to turn the situation to account in a way that captivated his heart. He engaged the servants to remain, and lost no time in striking a bargain with Mr. Craig, by which he agreed to pay the rent for a certain period, which Raish had left in arrear, and also to retain the house until the first of October, at an increased rate, on condition that part of the money was to go to Justin. This being settled, he went again to Tiverton, and threw himself upon the compassion of his young friends there. He was entirely alone, he said, and wanted some one to take charge of the house and banish the reminiscences of Raish which, otherwise, would haunt him there. Would they not come down and occupy it? All he wanted for himself was his present room, and perhaps a breakfast: most of the time he should be elsewhere. He represented, modestly, that it would be a great favor to him, if they would come.

"Ah," said Justin, with a tremble of ready sentiment in his young voice, and putting his hands on Oliphant's two shoulders, "if you weren't so much older than I, I should call you the most delicious, friendly fraud I ever knew. Of course we see through you — don't we, Vivian?" and he turned to her for the quick corroboration of which he was sure. "But as long as it's a delightful plan, and you've been guilty of a deception, I shouldn't wonder if we were to punish you by accepting it."

They did accept. They came down that evening; and there in his old home, with his old piano, Justin made the keys warble like a choir of birds, and filled Oliphant with generous satisfaction at the pleasure he had been able to bestow and the gladness that was given him in return. How like a dream it seemed! Only two months ago he had sat in the same place listening to Justin, and thinking of his apparently hopeless passion for Vivian Ware; and now she was here as Justin's bride. It was a happy omen; for at that time he had thought of Octavia, too, and at this moment he was thinking of her again!

It was several days since he had been able to see her, and he was resolved upon going to High Lawn on the morrow. He wanted to tell her how nicely the two young people were provided for; he wanted to tell her — but why go over it in advance? He knew perfectly well what he wished to say; and yet, on reflection, he didn't know very clearly. It eluded him in the most singular manner. The only thing was to go and see if it would elude him in Octavia's presence.

Before starting out, in the morning, he asked Vivian if she had any message for Octavia, in case he should see her; but doubtless the young wife would have guessed whither he had gone, without that. And when, all day, he did not make his appearance, she and Justin could not help thinking that the interview had resulted in something of unusual importance.

Oliphant went on foot, and every step seemed to make him lighter and more buoyant, instead of causing effort. The old song was humming itself in his brain, for the first time in a long interval: —

> "An' I were as fair as she,
>   Or she were as kind as I;" —

and it had a new significance now, though it carried him back to the day when he first saw Octavia. As he reached the small gate admitting to a side-path that led up to High Lawn, another sound greeted him, — a sound from without. It was the jangling chirr of the steel chains on Octavia's fleet horses, and for a moment Oliphant was troubled by the idea that she was just leaving the house; but the next instant he perceived that the carriage was approaching from the road above. Though he could not see it through the intervening English beeches, he heard it enter the drive, and knew that it swept up to the door, leaving a reminiscence of silvery tones in the air, which blended a wintry suggestion of sleigh-bells with the summer landscape.

He was exultant that she should have returned so in the nick of time to meet him; it flattered him with a fancy that some instinctive sense of his coming had called her home.

When he presented himself, the maid, with a confidence that augured well, said, "I think she is in;" then merely knocked at the half-open drawing-room door and announced his name. Octavia was within: she had just taken off her small, compact pansy bonnet, and held it in one hand by the strings, like a conventional shepherdess's flower-basket.

"Oh, then you didn't go away!" she exclaimed, coming forward with a dazzling welcome in her face, and what seemed to Oliphant a genuine air of relief. She shook hands with him cordially. "I had heard of Mr. Porter's downfall, and arrest, and all that," she said to him, rapidly; "and somehow I didn't feel sure that you would stay, don't you know? I thought his affairs might in some way affect you, — might make it necessary for you to go to New York."

"No, not at all," he returned, with unconscious dignity. "I had no connection with them but the accident of being in the house. And I certainly shouldn't have gone without letting you know."

How much or how little meaning he put into those last words was best known to Octavia. She slightly withdrew, as she heard them, and seated herself by the table, where she laid the minute basket-bonnet.

"I came near missing you," she proceeded, with a more subdued demeanor. "I have just this moment got back. Did you see me driving up? I went early to see Mrs. Chauncey Ware." The whole truth was that she had heard of Oliphant's taking the train the day before, and part of her errand this morning had been to find out casually, if she could, whether he had gone to New York or not. But of this she naturally said nothing. "You know," she continued, "the Wares were very indignant with both you and me, because they thought we had helped them to run away; I mean Vivian and Justin. So I determined to go down there and explain."

"Do you think it was worth while, if they choose to do us injustice?" asked Oliphant.

Octavia looked down, and blushed slightly. "I don't care so much for myself," she answered with hesitation. "I thought you would hardly care to speak for yourself, but that I might speak *of* you. Are you sorry?"

"No; I can't be, since you were taking that trouble on my account." If she had glanced up she would have seen that Oliphant was looking at her very gently.

"And I told Mrs. Ware that we certainly sympathized with the young people," she went on, eagerly, "and had hoped we should see them united."

"She'll be convinced of that," Oliphant remarked, rather defiantly, "when she hears what I have done." He went on, then, to tell her about it.

Octavia gave him an arch look; there was a sparkle of approbation in her eye, and her lips were touched with a mirthful sympathy. "Oh, yes," she cried, "now you've injured yourself with Mrs. Ware, beyond recovery! I'm so glad!"

"Oh, that's cruel — rejoicing in my misfortune," said Oliphant.

"I didn't mean *that*," Octavia answered. "You know: for the sake of Vivian and Justin." And she laughed at her mistake, so brightly and gayly that Oliphant felt he had never until then been upon such safe and easy terms with her.

"Then I'm not irretrievably ruined with you and Mrs. Craig," he said contentedly. "By the way, Vivian sent her love to you."

He failed in trying to utter this carelessly. A deeper chord stirred in his voice, and Octavia felt that it was the forerunner of something momentous.

"Thanks; and please give her mine, Mr. Oliphant," she returned, with downcast eyes. There was still a pure, fine color in her cheeks. She turned half away, to touch and smell some flowers upon the table; and it seemed as if while she inhaled their fragrance the glow of their beauty was reflected in her face.

He was about to speak, when that sense of knowing her so well and being on easy terms, which had just encouraged him, departed; and he felt that he hardly knew her at all. He beheld her loveliness; he could sit there and carry on ordinary conversation, as her acquaintance or friend; but what presumption had brought him to suppose that he could ever go below that fair surface? He experienced the terror which is not fear, but awe, that all finely strung natures are subject to, the moment they surrender to a great emotion.

"Mrs. Gifford," he began, after trying to steady himself against it, "do you know what has happened to me, while we have been watching those two young hearts — those friends of ours?"

If a clear glance, free from all flaw of suspicion, could have disarmed him, he would have been disconcerted then; for she responded with just that sort of glance, and the unperturbed expectancy of a child.

Perhaps it was not very certain in Oliphant's mind whether or not she made any definite answer; but the chance was his again to speak.

"I have grown to love you," he said, swiftly, with suppressed fervor. And all the while the strange awe of that master-passion was upon him and controlled him.

Did she, too, feel it? For an instant she covered her face with her hands. When she took them away, she was pale; the magic of the roses had vanished from her cheeks, and her apparent calm was maintained with difficulty.

"You, Mr. Oliphant?" There was a trembling hesitancy, a bewitching seductiveness, in her tone. "Ah, why? And how was I to know?"

"One doesn't find a reason for love, Mrs. Gifford. I only know that it is here in me, and is stronger than I am, and that you created it. May I not bring back to you what you have created?"

Like a woman luxuriating in some delicious melody, familiar but long unheard, Octavia reclined slightly in her fastidiously patterned chair, drinking in what he said.

"Is it possible," she murmured softly, "that I have been the cause of this — in so short a time, Mr. Oliphant?"

"But consider how rapidly we came to know each other," he urged, "and how much has happened in that time."

"Yes, yes," she mused aloud, sympathetically. "It has been very swift, and strange."

"More than that," he returned. "It has changed the whole current of my life: I know what it is, again, to be happy. We have had the same thoughts and the same interests, and every thing has seemed to bring us into closer relation, all the time. Haven't you found something in all this, too, Mrs. Gifford — and something that makes what I tell you now only natural?"

"Our friendship has given me a great deal of pleasure," said Octavia, still enjoying the luxury of receptiveness.

"But it is time for it to end!" he declared, boldly. "With me it *has* ended, because love has begun. Oh, I know, Mrs. Gifford, I have little enough to offer. I'm not rich, and I'm not brilliant or distinguished; but if I were, those things, after all, wouldn't be the chief. I could only offer you myself and my honest devotion, as I do now."

While he spoke he had risen; and there he stood with hands clasped tight together — a figure so much stronger than his words, so frank and determined yet reverent, that Octavia became aware of having underestimated the force of which he was capable. She nerved herself.

"You make too little of your merit, Mr. Oliphant. It is not a small thing to offer sincerely what you do. But why choose me? Why am I more worthy of it than some one else?"

"Why?" echoed Oliphant, with an intonation that bordered on a wondering laugh. "Because there can't be any one else, beside you! How can you think so for a moment?"

"I could scarcely help the question," she answered. "I was only thinking how easily there might be some spirit much younger and fresher than mine — some one who could give you all that your devotion would deserve. Consider, Mr. Oliphant: is there no one like that, whom you know?" Josephine was in her mind; and, while she flattered herself that she was giving Josephine a chance, she was really extracting the last drop of satisfaction from Oliphant's homage.

"It is a torture to me even to have you suggest such a thing," he declared, with vehemence. "Do you imagine that I have looked about me deliberately, and made my choice by a cold calculation? My sentiment for you is spontaneous, and I had hoped that you might have the same towards me. But you hesitate and reflect and question. . . . If it is not spontaneous, if it requires an effort" . . .

"You misunderstand me," Octavia hastened to assure him, though speaking quite low. Her hold upon her own purpose was weakening; she feared that he might drift away from her. "I like you very much — as a friend."

It did not surprise her, nor seem at all ridiculous, to see him drop on one knee before her. "You *will* care for me in the other way!" he cried, taking her hand. "I'm not ashamed to ask your compassion. You know my wretched loneliness, the emptiness of my life; but I have held myself together and existed — I never knew for what, until I met you. But now that I have allowed myself this hope of you, if it is taken away my loneliness and wretchedness will be twice what they were before. I am dependent on you."

"You are sure you have not deceived yourself?"

she asked in long-drawn tones, that intimated a refinement of yearning rather than any doubt or reluctance.

"No, a thousand times!" he exclaimed, with joyous energy. "I ask you to be my wife, my veritable wife — the woman I love with a strength beyond any thing I ever felt before! You will consent, Octavia?"

For the first time he had uttered, without prefix or addition, her name: that strange, arbitrary, yet coveted password to the closest intimacy, which is so easily seized, but so inoperative unless held by the right person.

He fixed his eyes upon her, and she gave back his gaze unfalteringly. I don't think she was certain, even then, whether she would accept or reject him. For a moment she permitted him all the sweetness of a realized conquest: he believed that he had won her. He saw an unwonted flashing in her eyes; a warm light that alternately advanced and retreated. As it came forward — that shifting light — and was concentrated on him, it seemed to be the glow of love. When it retreated, it grew uncertain; it was something else.

He rose, drawing her hand along with his, as if to lift her also and clasp her to him. She, too, began to rise, but as she did so she released her hand; the brilliance in her eyes retired, and yet filled them with an illumination the whole character of which was changed. She had recalled her determination. She remembered the hour when, in that very room, amid all those soft colors and those dainty surroundings, she had undergone an agony of which Oliphant had been the immediate agent.

Unaccountable, unnatural, though we may think it, the impulse of revenge which that crisis had excited had gone on persisting through her mutations of feeling about Oliphant, and revived at this instant, overcoming every other consideration. There the mood was, at any rate; and Oliphant had to take its consequences, no matter how little logic or mercy it had in it.

"No!" she said, abruptly. "I don't consent. I cannot."

"Not consent? How can you say that, now? And why? What has happened, to change you from a moment ago?"

"I'm not changed: I am steadfast," answered Octavia, almost fiercely, tossing her head slightly as though to shake off some imaginary restraining touch. "I never meant to take you! I have given no promise — not the least word."

"Then why did you let me go so far? Why have you gone so far yourself?" Oliphant demanded, in sudden, fiery remonstrance. "Why couldn't you have told me so at once?"

"I might have," she retorted, with a light, icy laugh. "But it would have cut short an agreeable acquaintance. It wasn't I who made any advance, Mr. Oliphant. *You* were the active one. And might I inquire why *you* have gone so far, if you don't like the inevitable result?"

"Because," Oliphant flung back, stingingly — "because I trusted you. Because I was unsuspicious, and took it for granted that you had a sense of honor.

Because I was candid with you from the start, and placed myself, just as I was, unreservedly in your hands."

"At your time of life you should have known better," said Octavia, with a mocking compassion. "Is it for a woman always to take care of a man, or of all men, and protect *them* from distress, as well as herself? I thought you would understand, of course, that I might be drawn on by the charm of such perfect attention as yours; naturally, I might continue to receive it as long as you thought it worth while to give it."

"Then you have done every thing deliberately?" he replied, inferentially.

"Why not, Mr. Oliphant?" She made a lazy, waving gesture with one hand. "It gave me pleasure. Didn't it you, too?"

"O my God! O Octavia!" he moaned, unthinkingly bringing together in speech the two powers — one divine, the other how sadly human! — that controlled his fate at this juncture. "And is this the end?" He appeared dazed, for an instant; then a fresh glow of hope came to him. "I don't know why it is," he said, half distraught, "but it seems to me that you are hardly in earnest. You will reconsider. You had some reason for wanting to test me; but you don't mean all that you have said. For Heaven's sake, tell me that you don't! You saw what was coming; you could so easily have sent me away; but you did not do it, and you gave me so much encouragement."

Octavia watched him as impassively as she might have done if he had been a curious automaton. One arm rested on the holly mantel, and her head leaned towards it: from her pallid face the eyes shone with a still coldness only less hard than that of her diamond ear-drops, which Oliphant now thought of always as the petrifaction of tears; and her long dress had swept round her in heavy folds that suggested a serpentine coil, so that she suddenly portrayed herself to him as a sorceress rising in the shape of woman from a lower half that was monstrous.

"You have deceived yourself, Mr. Oliphant," she answered, sweetly and calmly. "A few weeks ago we were strangers, but peculiar circumstances brought us together. You are trying to take advantage of them — that's all."

She saw an acute pain leap out and flood his face, as it were, altering it instantaneously. There is such a thing as spiritual bloodshed. A changed light of suffering flows out over the countenance of one who has been stabbed by words, as distinctly and with an effect as terrible as that of the scarlet life-tide which gushes from a physical wound.

"I must apologize humbly for my mistake," Oliphant said. "It was a great oversight." He cast about him briefly, with a despair that quickened into frenzy. "How dreadful it must be for you," he cried, "to be afflicted with this sort of mistake! But if you have done as I begin to think you have; if you have only trifled; if you have gone on purposely to inflict punishment on a sincere affection, then I can tell you this, Mrs. Gifford — you never loved, and you don't know what love is! But, no matter what you have done, *I* love you still, with a senseless infatuation, and, as I began by being frank, I can say to you now, if it gives you any satisfaction, that the blow you have given me is bitter — bitterer than death!"

He turned to go to the door.

Octavia did not yet relent. "Yes, it may be bitter," she said, keenly; "but other men have been rejected before now, and it was bitter to them, too, I suppose."

Instantly, the whole scheme of her vengeance became plain to him, then. He flashed one look at her, that told her so, and made her aware of her littleness.

This, and her woman's desire still to be thought well of — to do a wrong, yet somehow be assured that she was in the right — dissolved her firmness. She started from her contemplative attitude.

"What have I done? Oh, what have I said, Mr. Oliphant, that I ought not to? If I have caused you pain, will you not forgive me?"

Perhaps the dumb animal that we strike, in our power, forgives; but its piteous eyes accuse us still. For two or three moments, Oliphant remained mute; and the sight of him as he was then filled Octavia with horror of herself. His lips were steady, and not a muscle of his face moved, yet every heart-beat seemed to send a pulsation of anguish across it.

"Forgive?" he repeated at length, with something like contempt for an idle question. "Your request does me honor, Mrs. Gifford. Of course, it's a man's proudest prerogative to forgive."

A grim, curt laugh escaped him, and he made his way quickly out of the house.

XVI.

LITTLE EFFIE.

OLIPHANT'S most poignant anguish assailed him after he had left Octavia. He smarted with exasperation at the absolute rebuff he had received; but, beyond that, and still more sharply, he writhed under a sense of the weakness which had made it possible to expose himself to such humiliation and despair, for the sake of a mere fatuous illusion, a baseless dream, that had cost him all his peace of mind and his slowly acquired resignation to circumstances.

He was not resigned, now, you may believe. There was a snapping and a tingling in his veins, all over his body; his brain was tortured by an insufferable heat. It is no exaggeration to say that invisible furies seemed to accompany him and lash him with their whips, as he went along; for this Oliphant, beneath the peaceful, proper, and eminently modern blankness of his outward man, carried capacities for the utmost stress of emotion.

When he reached the gate of the drive he found it impossible to go towards the town. A wrathful, unqualified disgust for Newport had taken possession of him: he felt that his whole sympathy with the place had been a factitious and temporary one, and had suddenly fallen away from him. There was something false in the life; there was something false in Octavia: it all hung together. He walked away blindly towards the long, rolling moorland that lay between High Lawn and the ocean; he leaped a fence, and strode on through the midst of a light, gathering fog, — alone and miserable, yet glad to have his misery to himself. It was a region of low, rough-featured hills, or gradual swells, with ridges of gray rock pricking their way through the surface here and there, and showing in their spiny course like the dorsal fins of some impossible subterrene sort of fish. It was a region bleak, barren, and forsaken, the sight of which accorded with his wretched state of mind. Wandering on, he came at last to where he could look out upon the ocean, close by that spot where he and Octavia had gone down together to the Pirate's Cave; and there he heard the strange variations of an alarum from the steam fog-horn at Beaver Tail, which blew its colossal goblin tones mysteriously through the pale, shrouding vapor that overhung every thing around him. Though meant as a warning, to him it brought temptation: it was like the unearthly voice of an evil spirit, calling him on to he knew not what. Then, abruptly, the fog lifted a little, and revealed the patient, waiting sea: the thought of refuge and surcease from grief filled his mind. Yes, that was the meaning of the temptation: the weird voice through the mist was inviting him to suicide. Oliphant was not a swimmer, and one plunge from that rocky ledge by the cave, where he had held

•

his earlier memorable conversation with Octavia, would have meant, for him, speedy and painless death. Although naturally religious, he was not formally so, and had no scruple on that account against voluntary death; but he despised the weak violence of suicide, in a healthy being, both as a cowardly thing and as an unfit interference with natural laws, more shocking than the most hideous result of those laws. All the greater was his horror now, when the desire to end his life began to fasten itself upon him. He struggled hard with the fearful thought; but he did not dare stay where it assailed him in such palpable shape. He faced about, and walked swiftly across the rough downs again, this time making for the town; while the horn, which quavered incessantly up and down upon two hoarse and lamentable tones, hooted after him in evil derision.

Frequently he paused, or sat down on some knoll or rock, and lost himself in undefined revery, or sheer vacancy of numbness and desolation. He never knew quite how he passed the day; but he found that it was near dark when he came along Bellevue Avenue, on the way home. Just by Touro Park he suddenly encountered Roger Deering, and was surprised by it because he had not know that his cousin was in Newport. They both stopped for a rapid exchange of greetings, but both were too pre-occupied to notice at the time what recurred to them later. Roger was red-faced, short-haired, restless as usual, but there was something about him that made him look a changed man. And he himself had a curious impression that

Oliphant's hair had grown gray, but discovered that it was only that Oliphant looked so much older.

"When did you come?" asked Oliphant.

"Only to-day. Little Effie is very ill. I've just been again to look for the doctor."

"Ah," said Oliphant vaguely. "What is the matter?"

"Diphtheria," said Roger. The reply left no definite effect on Oliphant's mind; and the two men parted nervously, in haste, taking opposite directions.

Justin and his wife were waiting dinner for their friend; and, among other blissful little diversions of talk, they chatted about Oliphant. His long absence convinced them that he had made his offer, which they were expecting, to Octavia, and had been successful; but they allowed themselves some good-natured laughter at having, in their own case, got so far ahead of those older lovers. At last, when they heard the click of Oliphant's key in the hall door, Justin hurried out to meet him, but shrank back on seeing how haggard the widower was.

"You look ill," Justin said, anxiously. "You have tired yourself out, some way, haven't you? What can we do?"

Oliphant laid down his hat, and seemed unable to speak, for a moment. He moved unsteadily. "A glass of wine, please," he presently answered. "I am exhausted — have had nothing to eat since morning."

The wine refreshed him, and he soon joined the young couple, at dinner; but he was very grave and absent-minded. The only thing of importance that he said was, "I fear I shall have to leave you very shortly, Craig. I must go to New York — yes, complications have arisen that make it necessary. I will explain it all, by and by. Nothing to be alarmed at. Meanwhile, you understand, I shall keep every thing going here, just the same, of course; and it will oblige me if you and Mrs. Craig will keep an eye on it for me."

He could not inform them definitely when he should leave; in fact, he had not yet really formed any clear plan. But the events of the following two or three days settled this for him.

The next morning he was at first uncertain whether he had dreamed of meeting Roger, or had actually seen him; but as the fact became clear to him, he remembered that something had been said of Effie's illness: so he went down to the Deerings' small cottage, to make inquiry about it. Great were the astonishment and concern with which he learned that the child was very dangerously attacked, and that the doctor already considered her situation critical.

"I'm more sorry than I can tell you," said Oliphant to Roger. "But at least it's fortunate that you are here."

"I was called by telegraph," Roger answered, in an inert, hopeless tone. "But what can I do, now I'm here? It is these fatal unsanitary conditions that have done the harm; and as for us, we are helpless — at the mercy of the disease, if it has any mercy. Ah, if we had only not come to Newport!"

Oliphant started at the reproduction, in those words,

of the thought which was passing through his own mind with regard to himself.

"Well, old man, let's try to keep up hope," he said, forlornly seeking to throw some cheer into his words, yet knowing that he failed dismally.

"Yes," said Roger. He looked wanly at his cousin, with an effort to express gratitude by his look. "But somehow, Eugene, I feel pretty sure that I shall never feel those little arms around my neck again."

Roger moved suddenly towards the window, leaned one arm upon the sash, and bent his head low, as if gazing attentively out of the window. He was really sobbing.

Oliphant recalled how, not many days before, he had been with Mary Deering and her baby daughter, when Effie was commanded, for some reason, to go out of the room. "What because?" asked the little toddling girl, beginning to pucker her lips; and he had laughed at the phrase, which was a frequent one with her; and the mother, being equally smitten by it, had caught up Effie, cuddled and embraced her, and sent her away with a smile of perfect contentment on her tiny, roseate features. "What because?" He fancied he heard the words at this instant, pronounced in her sweet, wavering treble, with just a suspicion of innocent protest in it; and it was strange how they answered to the sad wonderment in himself, at the misery that had befallen him and the awful suspense in which he beheld his cousins placed. But there was no watchful motherly power that could come to the relief of any of *them*, and dissipate their woes.

"Of course she is conscious," he hazarded, hoping in some way to relieve the father. "She knew you when you arrived, didn't she?"

Roger roused himself, and spoke firmly, though his eyes were moist: "Oh, yes; she said 'Papa,' once. I believe they are always conscious."

That word "they," relegating her to a general class, in a region somewhere beyond the reach of human help; recognizing her as already caught up into the arms of God — to be borne away or restored, who could tell? — made Oliphant quiver with a new consciousness of the poor fellow's terrible position. "I do hope, Roger," he said, "if there's any thing I can do, you'll let me know. Mary mustn't wear herself out."

"She will never leave Effie, Eugene," Roger replied. "Did I tell you she was up all night? Never mind, my dear fellow. It is hard for you that you can't help us, I know; but — I will send for you if — if there is any thing of importance."

Oliphant could not trust himself to stay any longer, then. "I shall come again this evening," he said hurriedly, and took his departure.

The voiceless contest went on at the little cottage all day. Even Clarence was subdued; he crept unobtrusively about the house, and did not know what to make of the situation, except that the world began to appear to him a very different sort of place from what he had supposed it. During the afternoon hours the usual crush and sparkle of the driving throng filled Bellevue Avenue. In the quiet of this interior, Mary could hear the genteel rumble and patter of the horses and carriages not far away: the parade of Anglo-maniacs and distorted grooms, of beaming beauties and insolently handsome young men and high-stepping steeds, was in full progress. But to the anxious mother the thought of that spectacle had lost all its glamour; the whole concourse, indeed, assumed to her fancy the likeness of a grotesquely pompous funeral train.

Night came, and still there was the same scene in the room where Effie lay: a childish form prostrate on the bed, feverish and suffering, with golden hair spreading at random over the pillow — the face already grown singularly mature with a knowledge of the awful possibilities of pain; and three figures — the mother, the father, and the nurse — that went and came often, with noiseless, imperceptible movements, ministering continually, and uttering words of soothing that could not be replied to. For the little thing was now scarcely able to speak, and had all that she could do to breathe.

Atlee had called during the day, and had been informed, at the door, of the illness. Now he came again, early in the evening; but he saw no one excepting the servant, who reported his coming, after he had gone, to Roger and Mary, just then resting for a few minutes in another room. On the mention of his name, husband and wife gazed silently at each other, and significantly. As yet, no discussion had been raised between them regarding Atlee, and of course they said not a word at this juncture; but Mary Deering sent up a brief, disconnected, unspoken prayer to heaven, for pardon of the folly which seemed now almost too senseless to require pardon. She understood so little of Providence that she considered her present trial as a direct personal punishment for the apparent wrong she had done Roger; and she imagined that a passionate inward avowal of her misdemeanor might be answered by the saving of her child.

Oliphant and Justin arrived later; and the former settled himself to wait below throughout the night, in case he should be needed. Hour after hour, in the room above, the scene continued unchanged, except that for a long time the doctor was there, observing, thinking, issuing a few directions, and at last going away without imparting any hope. A medicinal pastil was burning slowly on a little side-table; the air of the room could not be freed from a certain deadly closeness; the three figures continued at their post, with a still, concentrated energy, a peculiar exaltation of devotedness, as if they were athletes engaged in a struggle too intense to admit of words. Effie remained nearly motionless; the dry crepitation of her tortured breath emphasized the hush of the room, by its regular iteration. And hour after hour the plain little interior grew more sacred as a centre of parental love, while the man and woman to whom that imperilled life was dear watched its fading, and inhaled the poisonous atmosphere around them without fear of the danger that it threatened to them.

Once, when Effie was to take a prescribed potion, she roused herself, and looked around as if searching for aid, or for some explanation of the awful combat in which she was forced to engage. The voice which had been so long nearly stifled found its way through the choking barrier in her throat, and she gasped painfully, "What because?"

At length, near the morning, she rose on her couch, and called clearly for her mother. The final moment had come, though Roger and Mary, misled by the last bright flicker of the vital flame, fancied at first that she was reviving. Suddenly, the signs of dissolution set in. The child continued sitting up, and the father and mother each held one of her hands, looking anxiously towards her, striving still to give her some comfort. She turned her eyes, large and bright with a new intelligence, first to one and then to the other: but presently their lustre began to dim; her strength waned; there passed from her fingers to each of the hands in which they rested three quick, fluttering pulsations, that did not stir the surface, but seemed to thrill electrically from the interior sources of the little life. The father and mother instinctively met one another's gaze, and without a syllable, recognized that they had received the last greeting of a spirit about to depart. In the midst of their agony, this mysterious communication gave them one instant of supreme perception — a perception that afterwards lived in their memories tinged by emotion which, paradoxically, was like a holy joy.

Then Effie sank back, breathless, quiet; calm, calm forever; rigid in lifelessness, yet lying as light upon the bed as a drift of newly fallen snow. The white truce upon her face proclaimed surrender and peace.

All night the wind had been sweeping to and fro,

bringing together the elements of a storm. When Roger, in the weird, gray gleam of the dawn-light, slipped noiseless as a ghost into the narrow parlor where Oliphant waited, the storm burst in a torrent of rain ; and the trees before the house, bending in the wind, swayed their dark-draped branches with gestures of grief and abandonment.

XVII.

REPENTANCE.

NOW that the fatal blow had fallen upon Roger and Mary, which their friends would so gladly have strained every faculty to prevent, Oliphant and Justin found that they could help. It is the sad privilege of human beings, at such times, to come when all is over and prove their own essential uselessness by performing every possible act of practical and tender aid in those details that cover up the death in our hearts, as dust is made to cover the actual dead. Yet in seasons of the greatest grief at a personal loss, the things we most prize are the seemingly useless ones — sweet, ineffectual flowers, a few helpless words, expressing the sorrow of those whom we love, that they cannot do any thing for us.

Vivian was quick in seconding her husband and his friend to give what assistance they could; for, although she had hardly known Mary Deering, her loyalty to the friendship of Oliphant brought into action her natural fervor of sympathy as a young wife for the stricken mother. Josephine, too, carried flowers to the door of the house of mourning. Oliphant was there at the time, and when the box was opened an impulse led him to hurry to the porch, whence he saw Josephine herself moving quickly away down the shaded street. It touched him that she had chosen to bring the flowers in her own hands.

But nothing was heard from Octavia; she made no sign; so far as Oliphant could tell, she might have been totally in ignorance of the catastrophe.

Yet how could she do any thing? She had thrown Oliphant aside in such a way as to preclude every relation, henceforth, except that of the most distant recognition. She had had but very slight intercourse with Mary Deering, and it would have been mainly because of her constant association with Oliphant during the season that she would have made, if at all, any demonstration of condolence. Therefore, she was entirely debarred from showing her sympathy. She felt a great sympathy, nevertheless. I do not care to analyze the sources of it, because injustice would certainly be done in trying to formulate a state of mind requiring so delicate a balance to weigh it, as hers did. But I am sure that genuine womanly compassion and kindness were uppermost in her mood. In presence of this tragedy, too, a sharp light fell upon her recent conduct, which brought out with terrifying distinctness its ugliness and cruelty. She began to be remorseful.

She did form a plan of sending some flowers to Mrs. Deering, anonymously; but the conclusion soon followed that such a course would be cowardly, and merely an attempt to narcotize her conscience. Then, hearing that funeral services were to be held over poor little Effie at old Trinity, she resolved to go thither and attend them. But from this as well she was restrained, by a conviction that she had no right to do it. "Why should I take advantage of this dreadful sorrow," she said to herself, "under the pretence that a generous feeling of pity makes me set aside my personal affair with Mr. Oliphant?"

And so she sat wretchedly alone at High Lawn, unable to take any step, and suddenly deserted by those who had lately been nearest to her. Josephine did not approach her, and Perry Thorburn had not come to see her, for some time past. It did not need these things, however, to give her a true comprehension of her pitiful error. Just then when she sprang forward and asked Oliphant to forgive her, before he left the house, the first seed of repentance had sprung up in her mind, stirred to life though it was by a false impulse of vanity and conceit. But repentance had multiplied in her, since, from a hundred other germs; and before she heard of Effie's illness at all, her heart was aching for Oliphant. She was disgusted with herself; she utterly repudiated what she had done at the prompting of a vindictive whim, that now appeared hardly less than insane.

Tragic events often come in such a way that, while they seem to bring about certain moral changes in us, and we therefore refer such changes to what we call a mere "accident," those events are really only the afterclap, or the tangible symbol, of what has already taken place in our minds.

Of course I do not know why Effie died just at that time; but I am perfectly clear that Octavia's repentance, which was emphasized and stimulated by this disaster, was in no manner a consequence of it.

The day came for the services at Trinity. The storm had cleared; there was an exultant, cool vigor in the air. Very few people, naturally, attended; but it had been an ardent wish of Justin's that, if any obsequy were held in Newport, it should be where he could offer his farewell to the lost spirit of the child, in music. And he played the Raindrop Prelude, which stole gently through the church with a sweet, dewy freshness and simplicity, yet fell plaintively upon the listeners, and made them think of gentle tears shed in a loving resignation. Oliphant remembered too well how he had heard that melody before; and as it had brought to his mind then the refreshing showers of summer, it now suggested the sad drops of autumn, that patter down a requiem for dead hope.

The coffin was carried out. Oliphant waited for a brief space, and as he made his way to the street he met Josephine Hobart. "Mr. Oliphant," she said, "I want to say to you — though it may seem unusual, coming from a stranger almost, as I am — how much I feel for your cousins. Their loss has gone to my heart more than any thing that has happened for many a day. It must have been a great blow to you, too."

"Yes," he answered; "I don't know why, but it is to me like losing a child of my own."

I suppose she must have read the secret of his other loss. Her large, soft, unrevealing eyes were filled with a stilly, comprehensive look of fellowship.

"You are going with them to New York?" she asked.

"Oh, yes."

"And sha'n't we see you in Newport again?"

Oliphant's face grew vague and listless, for an instant. "I'm afraid not: I don't believe I shall come back," he said.

He had not admitted this to the Craigs.

Before he left her he thanked her for her gracious act of bringing the flowers. They shook hands, and the unconscious trembling of her touch roused in him, transiently, an undefined wonder at the stress of her sensibility, which he attributed wholly to the death of Effie Deering. But as he went to join his cousins at the New York boat, his mind was on Octavia and the dreariness of the fact that she was not with him, sharing the piteous solemnity of this hour, in which even the glad young love of Justin and Vivian had participated.

Oliphant's care had smoothed the way for Roger and Mary, by putting out of sight the rougher details of the journey; but the night-voyage to New York was a melancholy one for them all. They glided away, however, and were lost in a moment to the gay, pleasure-seeking little world in which they had lately been active. Octavia heard the great boat go by, with its throbbing hum of strong paddle-wheels, and knew that it was taking her honest, defeated lover away from her — perhaps forever; but it was too late to recall him, then. In a few minutes the sound of the departing steamer ceased to vibrate upon her ear: she was left to the desert silence which she had made for herself.

Change and catastrophe had overtaken several of the people about whom this story centres; but it must not be supposed for an instant that such disturbances of mere feeling or fortune affected in the least the dazzling monotony of festal existence in the society around them. It is true, Dana Sweetser seized upon the untimely demise of the Deerings' child as a potent case in point to fortify his position regarding drainage. Sundry physicians insisted that the fatal malady was directly due to the absence of good hygienic conditions. Sundry others, supported by a large number of people who had not yet died, disputed the proposition. Every one agreed that it was very sad for the Deerings; and industrious correspondents, who habitually wrote and telegraphed catalogues of visitors and distinguished dining-room tattle to leading journals, dropped a sentence or two of rose-water pathos on Effie's bier. All the proprieties were observed, and nothing was done to better the drainage; so Dana Sweetser fell back temporarily on the Alaska and British Columbia Inlet Excavation.

One result of the discussion was that the Deerings were elevated to a social importance, in the way of talk, which they themselves had never enjoyed. They were utilized with soup, at dinners, as an introductory topic, or as a relish with the *hors d'œuvres;* by dessert, however, they ceased to be mentioned; and in two or three days their misfortune was dismissed entirely.

But Octavia could not so easily get rid of the things which had lately happened. Her time was in demand for many engagements, day and night, and she moved in the thickest of the whirl. Oliphant being out of the way, moreover, various discouraged gentlemen, who had stood at a distance while he was present, began to crowd round her again. Perry Thorburn likewise suddenly returned to her society, and asked her to drive with him, every day, although he hardly spoke to her of Josephine, any longer. Notwithstanding all this, and the sparkling exterior which she maintained, her inward distress deepened. When alone, she was moody and dispirited ; no employment sufficed to calm her restless thoughts ; she spent hours reviewing her association with Oliphant and her conduct towards him. At last she paid her intended visit to Vivian, which she had been deferring out of dread at meeting the keen eyes of Oliphant's friends, who would be so quick to detect the change that had come over her, and her responsibility for the change in him. At first she tried to discover when Oliphant was likely to return ; but before she left Vivian, she had made a partial confession of the true state of things, though with important reservations. She admitted that Oliphant had proposed for her hand, and that she had sent him away without hope ; but she did not tell of the poisonous thrusts she had given him.

"I'm so sorry," said Vivian, looking up from a little drawing she was making for Justin — "so sorry for poor Mr. Oliphant;" then she added, her blue eyes scanning the widow's face for an instant with complete but kindly insight, "and sorry for you, too, Octavia."

"For me?" Octavia blushed faintly, and moved her head so that only the dainty profile of her face came within Vivian's range.

"Yes," answered the bride. "I can't help saying so. He is such a sterling man. Of course I don't attempt to judge for you, but I think you may regret, some time, what you have done."

"But do you approve of second marriages?" Octavia rejoined, quickly. "Would *you* be willing" . . .

"No," said Vivian, promptly. "At least," she continued, putting another touch to her sketch, "I can't conceive of myself in that position, and somehow I have a feeling against it. But then, true love is too great a thing to be bounded by my feeling, I am sure. It comes in so many different ways . . . And when it comes, one is in the hands of a higher power, which one ought to be very careful about trifling with."

Nothing more was said, for a few moments. Afterwards, they passed to the alienation of Vivian's mother and brother, which still continued. But while Octavia stood by the piano, making a final remark or two, Vivian casually resumed the subject of Oliphant. "It troubles me," she said, "that Mr. Oliphant doesn't come back. Let's see: it's three — no, four days, now. Justin wrote him a long letter, but we've only received one little note from him. He's staying at the Van Voort House, and I'm afraid he's too comfortable to be in a hurry about coming here again."

She laughed lightly, with an air of directing a sarcasm against her own housekeeping; but Octavia understood her. They kissed each other, as they parted.

Octavia went home and spent much of the day composing a short letter to Oliphant: —

MY DEAR MR. OLIPHANT, — I shall not wonder if you are surprised at hearing from me, for I feel that there would be no propriety in my writing to you, after what has happened between us — nor should I wish to do so — were it not for a single thing which no one but myself can tell you. And even I have discovered it only since you went from here.

That is, that I now see how wrong I was in my treatment of you, and how much injustice I did you by some of the things I said the last time we met. What led me on, it is hard to say exactly. I am not sure that I myself understand; but even if it were possible for me to unravel it all, perhaps you would rather spare me the mortification, if you had the choice.

You have been called away; it seems to be uncertain whether you will return here, and if you did so we should not be likely to meet, I suppose. This is why I consider it best to acknowledge my fault by writing. I do not ask you, Mr. Oliphant, to forgive — as I selfishly did, that day — but only to pardon me for not seeing sooner what I was drifting to, and preventing it. I cannot hope that you will think of me otherwise than with censure, or that I can ever recover the friendship I have sacrificed; but it is my duty to admit my mistake, and to assure you of my lasting respect.

Sincerely,
OCTAVIA GIFFORD.

After despatching this, she was more at peace with herself. Ever since Oliphant's departure, she had been undergoing one very peculiar form of nervous disturbance. The rotary beat of the steamer's wheels, with the transient pause and renewed throb as the engines turned them, kept sounding in her ears at the most inopportune times; and every morning, early, just before dawn woke the sky, sleep deserted her, and she lay waiting intently for the same sound to assure her that the boat from New York was returning.

At first it would steal to her from a distance, through the dusk, like a deep, unsteady breathing; gradually, and then more swiftly, it became defined as a regular and mighty pulsation, coming nearer, increasing in volume: it was what one might imagine to be the voice of a vast shadow. Finally, it developed into a systematic concussion, the nature of which was unmistakable. Octavia would rise, go to the window, and watch the vague white shape as it rounded Fort Adams like a floating town, with mysterious colored lights strung up at stem and stern and at various other points, or shining from the windows. There was something spectral about it, and the palpitation of the huge paddle-wheels was like a shudder. Involuntarily Octavia would shudder, too, and creep back to bed.

But to-night, since her letter had gone, she did not shudder when she woke and saw the boat. A soft warmth enveloped her heart, as if that spectral shape had been the forerunner of some great happiness destined to come to her in its wake.

XVIII.

THE NIGHT-VOYAGE.

WHEN Oliphant arrived at New York, the widespread rush and murmur of the city's activity repeated, in its different way, the buffeting and general troubled noise of the waves at Newport. He had escaped their haunting effect, only to find himself standing on the edge of a second, but human, ocean; and a leap into one seemed much the same as a leap into the other. He did not know where he was going, what he was to do henceforth: he had no purpose. To merge himself in this chafing tide of humanity, not knowing what was to be his future, struck him as little more than another mode of suicide, similar in its result to that of losing himself in the currents of the sea.

Putting up at the Van Voort House, he accompanied Roger and Mary in the final ceremony of laying Effie in Woodlawn Cemetery; then he went to his hotel and did nothing. The next day he made inquiries regarding a passage to Europe, and secured the refusal of a berth. Immediately afterwards he began planning a trip to California. In short, he was aimless. I don't know that it was his fault, especially. The present century, which overflows with the most pronounced aims of all sorts, probably harbors more people who find it impossible to have an aim than any century heretofore.

On the third day, he received a letter from Justin, detailing some roundabout approaches which had been made by Mrs. Chauncey Ware towards a reconciliation, together with incidental items of Newport news. Mrs. Ware had allowed semi-official information to be conveyed to Justin that she would recognize his marriage with Vivian if he would abandon the musical profession, and enter a certain banking-house where she could procure him a reasonably good position, with prospects of a partnership. Justin had said in reply, somewhat truculently, that his marriage was recognized by the church, and to some extent by mankind, and that he did not think he would make a very good banker; but that, if his mother-in-law would treat him with the courtesy he was prepared to offer her, he thought they could agree admirably. It appeared, furthermore, that Count Fitz-Stuart was believed to have ratified a treaty with Mrs. Farley Blazer, by which he consented to cede himself to Miss Ruth, in consideration of sundry state obligations, which the count had incurred, being assumed by Mrs. Blazer; and that the engagement of Lord Hawkstane and Miss Tilly Blazer had been announced.

With regard to the latter piece of gossip, Oliphant, who read Justin's communication in Roger's office on Exchange Place, observed, "The milk and water have coalesced at last. I don't know which dilutes the other the most."

Justin's allusions to his own affairs, however, set Oliphant thinking as to how he could help the boy; more particularly since Justin had remarked in his letter, "I have entered on a harder struggle than I foresaw, but I am not afraid."

He went to his lawyer, the very next morning. "I'm about to go away from New York," he said, "for an extended absence. There are some little things that ought to be arranged; and I think, to provide against accidents, I'd better make a new will."

The making of the will did not take long, but in it there was a provision for Justin. Oliphant did not expect that to be of any immediate use; but he wanted to lead up to an arrangement which he now proceeded to effect, whereby certain regular payments were to be made to Justin, in such a way that he could not avoid accepting them, ostensibly for aiding the continuance of his musical studies.

He also inquired of the lawyer about Raish, whose case he found had been set to come up before Judge Hixon, in the course of a month or so. "There won't be the ghost of a chance for him, I hear," said the legal adviser. "Great pity — not so much on his account, but for his excellent family connections. His relatives will feel it severely."

On returning to the Van Voort, he made up his mind to take the California trip: somehow, though he believed that he never should think of Octavia again without a repulsion that fell little short of animosity, he could not bring himself to leave the country while she was in it. And having come to this conclusion, he wrote and posted a letter to Justin, announcing his speedy departure; giving him also a general sketch of what had happened at his last visit to High Lawn.

The next afternoon's mail-delivery brought him the few lines that had been wrung from Octavia, the day before, by her silent self-reproaches. If this missive had come a few hours later, it would have failed to reach him, because, growing restless, he had determined to start that night for California. As it was, he read it, folded it up, and put it in his pocket with a slight sigh, and a recurrent pang of the first wretchedness which Octavia's refusal had inflicted upon him. He took it as one more evidence of the irony which had controlled his whole career, that she should not have come to her present state of mind until she had wrought irreparable havoc with him. Of what use was her repentance to him, now?

Before beginning to pack he read the letter a second time, preparatory to burning it. But, as he read, a sudden and wild thrill of renewed hope coursed through him. Octavia's words developed, as he thought, a double meaning. "I was wrong in my treatment of you. . . . Uncertain whether you will return here, and even if you did so we should not be likely to meet, I suppose." . . . Might not these phrases be a roundabout way of saying that she had erred in not accepting his love, and wished that he *would* return and see her? He could not reason about it; he only felt; and his recent conviction that Octavia had inspired in him a resentment amounting to hatred did not seem worth even passing notice. California became an impossibility; vanished, in short. It was imperative to get to Newport. Too late for the afternoon train, he telephoned for a state-room on the boat. Every room was engaged; but this only stimulated his eagerness to go. There was not much time remaining, and hastily packing up his things he took a coupé, drove down through the city to the wharves, and went on board the steamer, with the intention of staying up all night, or dozing in the big saloon.

Before the start, he met, in the crowd of many hundreds that was drifting about the loudly upholstered cabins, clogging the stairs, and packing itself away on the open decks, Perry Thorburn. "How did you come here?" exclaimed Oliphant.

"I had to run on for a day, on business," Perry explained, with a smile which only half concealed some unpleasant thought. He had really come to look into his affairs, and to perfect a scheme for making up as well as he could the losses his father had inflicted upon him. "The old man's on board, too. Got a room, have you?" he continued. "Awfully crowded to-night."

"No," said Oliphant; "but I'm in a hurry. I was just thinking I might have taken the late train and got off at Providence. The boat's cooler, though."

Perry offered him one of the berths in his stateroom, as he and his father were separate; but Oliphant declined it, rather liking the idea of being alone and of passing a sleepless night in revery upon his revived hopes.

Every thing seemed strangely beautiful and joyous

to him. As the boat swept around the Battery with easy, omnipotent motion, and steamed up East River, passing miles and miles of masonry on either side, lined by clustering ships whose spars and rigging rose in slim black lines against the background of dense brick or light sky, like the characters of some unknown language inscribed there, the scene stirred and elated him by its might of human interest. It soothed him, too. He knew what misery and squalor swarmed upon those river banks, and what anxious hearts beat in myriads behind the long front of populous buildings; but he felt that there was a dignity in the human struggle, which was intensified by the desperation of it, and redeemed much of the pettiness and evil. He had had his struggles, also, and could sympathize; besides, his present happiness filled him with a livelier sense of human brotherhood than he had felt for a long time.

The mellow light of a peaceful sunset that was approaching suffused with delicious radiance the smoky heaps of dull-toned architecture, and glimmered softly on the gray-green waters through which the steamer was ploughing. The city melted away like a dream; the Long Island shore crept off towards the outer ocean; the green banks of Connecticut, with rounded promontories and dim inlets, rolled by. The number of passengers on the decks diminished; the brass band, which had been blaring with a specious brilliancy at the after end of the saloon, ceased playing: Oliphant began to enjoy comparative solitude. Perry joined him for a while, and they went to supper with old Thorburn. Afterwards Oliphant and Perry smoked a cigar or two on the after-deck. Finally the widower was left entirely alone, and went forward to the upper deck at the bow.

It was night now. The stars were shining in great multitude and beauty; the golden points or crimson spots like fading coals, that marked the position of lighthouses on either coast, came out at irregular intervals, registering the progress of the voyage, then sank back into invisibility. The great steamer proceeded on her way with throb and beat and shudder; with her four decks — orlop, cabin, hurricane, main; with her double cordon of state-rooms arranged like a system of cells; with her masses of costly merchandise, her heterogeneous crowd of costly passengers; her colored lanterns that glowed above her like luminous insects of large size, hovering in the air and accompanying her movement. There was no stir of life upon her at this hour; and Oliphant, sitting close to the cabin wall, well wrapped up against the night chill, looked ahead over the dimly gleaming Sound, and meditated. He was very confident of his coming happiness; all his doubts were over; there was a bounding exultation in his blood. The frustrations and disappointments that had beset him all his life seemed to be at an end; he was sure that he was about to enter upon that period of contentment and enjoyable activity for the hope of which we all live. How absurd his passing thought of suicide, a few days before, must have seemed to him then!

The steamer went on: the broad, foamy wake behind her seemed to weave itself into a record of the forsaken past, and every pulsation of the engines was to Oliphant like the expectant beat of his own heart, moving towards a bright future. A thin shrouding of mist was drawn over the stars, after a while, which was occasionally dispersed, and then returned to dim the prospect. The steamer began blowing signals now and then from her pipes. Presently, signals in a similar tone were heard somewhere in advance; a vessel of the same line was approaching. The two damp and screaming voices seemed to establish an understanding, as the red and gold and green of the other boat's lights came into sight through the fog, like the gleaming eyes of a monster. She was steering to the right. Nevertheless, suddenly she changed her direction, swerved quickly around, and came swiftly towards the New York boat, head on.

There was a quick, excited ringing of engine-room bells; there was more blowing of whistles; but nothing served to avert the catastrophe. The Newport boat loomed up clearly in the fog, for an instant; and then there came a violent shock, followed by the ripping and tearing and groaning of rended wood. The New York boat's engines stopped; she was fatally wounded by the other, and floated helpless on the tide.

At once an indescribable tumult arose among her passengers. The saloon lights went out. Innumerable people burst forth from the state-rooms like resurrected bodies and ran madly hither and thither in their white garments, silent or with loud shrieks. The rush of scalding steam, escaping from the engine-room with a deep roar of release, partially muffled these cowardly cries, and strangled many of the flying figures; but the noise and tumult on board were strangely in contrast with the silence of the night that surrounded and shut in all this trouble like a vast and stilly tomb.

A few found life-preservers; others seized upon chairs, or doors, which they or some one else had wrenched off, no one knows how; and many who could swim leaped overboard without any thing to aid them in floating. Every thing that occurred, all the things that were done, occupied so short a space of time that the results did not seem to proceed from any conscious action. Countless heads of people, swimming, struggling, or drowning, were sprinkled in black dots on the water.

The steamer had lurched somewhat, but did not appear to be sinking. Immediately upon the collision, Oliphant had clambered up to the topmost deck, and had gone aft that way. Perry Thorburn, who, in the midst of a frantic, pushing throng on the open canopied deck just below, was looking vainly for his father, saw Oliphant leaning down and peering over from above. He shouted to him and pointed towards the water, and Oliphant nodded. Still, some minutes elapsed before he leaped: with many others who could not swim, he preferred to take the last chances on the doomed vessel. In a minute or two, however, after Perry had thrown himself from the rail, a twisted lance of flame burst from the boat's side: fire had broken out on board.

Perry was a good swimmer, and had struck out towards the other steamer, which, after recoiling from the shock, had sheered off, and was now getting out boats. But he paused very soon, treading water and turning to look again for his father. A quantity of broken timbers, boxes, and other buoyant objects were already drifting about in the water, and he found it advisable to get hold of one of these and rest a while. When the fire leaped forth, he pushed still nearer the wreck. The flames increased, and lit up the broad, liquid surface around him: it was then that he saw the bulky form of his father sliding down a rope, which he had evidently tied to a post and flung into the water. Perry began making his way in that direction. Old Thorburn had not much skill in swimming, but he succeeded in getting a little way out. He kept casting about for some artificial aid. Near him was a woman, with a small child in her arms, who, almost by a marvel, had got hold of a long bench, and was sustaining herself by it. Thorburn came up with her and caught at the wood, apparently much fatigued. The bench was not large enough to keep them both up: the woman expostulated.

Thorburn was wild with the danger of his situation. There was to him, no doubt, something unsurpassably outrageous in the idea that he, the owner of the steamer, with all his wealth, his power in Wall Street and among the railroads, his vast plans and teeming resources, should not only sustain an actual heavy financial loss by the accident, but should be put in peril of his life, struggling there in the salt tide like a common individual of the general public, or as if he were of no more account than a drowning rat. Small wonder if his heavy mouth grew fierce and his indignant eyes more belligerent than usual.

He began to pound the woman's hands unmercifully, in order to make her loose her hold.

Perry, who was still a good distance away, shouted to his father, sharply: "Don't do that, dad! Stop, I say! I'm coming." At the same time he was exerting every muscle to propel himself and his piece of flotsam to the spot.

It was virtual murder that was being attempted before his eyes, and the person who sought to destroy another's life was his own father! This Perry perceived clearly; and the sight of the deed and the thought of its awful significance were more abhorrent to him than any danger of engulfment and drowning that threatened himself. Words spoken by a man in the water are necessarily somewhat gasping and uncertain in utterance; and whether it was from this cause, or the plashing of the waves around him, or the increasing hum of the flames on the boat, or the conflict of cries from other throats, old Thorburn did not seem to hear his son's appeal. He continued to beat the helpless woman, encumbered by her child, and to tear her hands away from her accidental raft.

So unequal a contest could not last long. It was apparently but a few seconds before the unknown woman yielded, and dropped away from the frail support. But at that supreme juncture, with the fate of suffocation and death closing upon her, the heart of the mother was unselfish: it gave what might prove to be its final beating, its last impulse, to an effort on behalf of her still more helpless baby, who, benumbed by the unwonted situation, was not even conscious of the deadly peril. She lifted her child into the air as high as she could with one arm, while with the other she vaguely and instinctively sought to delay her sinking.

Just then Perry, who was drawing nearer, saw another dark mass approaching her, only a few feet away. It was a man, clinging to a broken timber. The man signalled the woman with a cry: "Here!" She heard him, and with a last desperate turn and bewildered floundering through the thick water she succeeded in grasping the means of rescue that he offered. That, also, was very slight; insufficient for the floating of two persons. But the man who had called to her scarcely waited to test it before he abandoned it entirely.

For an instant he lifted his face heavenward, as if gazing at the stars, which now beamed mildly down upon the fearful and glaring spectacle of the steamer in conflagration and her scattered victims; for the scurrying mists had disappeared. Ay, thus he fronted those stars, which Count Fitz-Stuart had wearily dismissed as being "so old," and Raish had adopted as figuring the glowing butts of cigars he had smoked. Then he cast himself off, and disappeared beneath the low-crested waves.

While the face was turned upward, however, the broadening wall of fire from the steamer's side had shed upon it a vivid illumination, and Perry had been able to recognize the man.

It was Oliphant.

"Oliphant, old boy!" he screamed with hoarse desperation. "Wait! Where are you?"

Where? Where indeed? no answer came, to Perry's shout. It was impossible to determine at the moment whether Oliphant rose again, or not; for, despite the ghastly distinctness of the scene, every thing that happened was rapid, confused, bewildering and almost unreal. The surface of the Sound seemed to have grown smoother, as if subdued by a terror of what was taking place. Perry swam close to the stranger woman, and began assisting her. Boats had begun to pick up some of the survivors. He could not bear to approach or even look at his murderous old father, who still puffed, fumed, and splashed, in his efforts to advance by means of the half-submerged bench. The flames poured roaring upward from the steamer, in deep volumes, wide belts, thick coils, volatile spirals — ruddy, crimson, or like melted gold — and the bones of the mighty structure were heard to crack as if she had been in the grasp of a fiery anaconda. Their terrific splendor was reflected in the flood so intensely, so universally, that Perry seemed to himself to be swimming through a burning lake of Hell.

Again came the question, where was Oliphant? Perry could not abandon the belief that, somehow or other, his friend had been rescued; yet the picture of that face looking starward was stamped upon his mind; he saw it subsiding into the vague, relentless wash of the waves. He imagined the stalwart but helpless figure of that quiet manly man going down, down, down into the silent, unknown depths; and he could feel, very nearly as if it were his own experience, the strangling sensation, the struggle against suffocation, the final dreamy resignation which, he had heard, accompany death by drowning.

Meanwhile, high over the weltering gleams, over the black eastward smoke of the burning bulk, and the quivering mirror of water that tremulously gave back a glow of red, the stars hung poised in eternal flight — calm, restful, yet distributed over the sky as capriciously as if they had just been lodged in their places by some haphazard volley from an exploded world.

XIX.

LOVE AT LAST.

DANA SWEETSER, whose great cares and responsibilities had aided in making the ravages of time more apparent upon his countenance, was engaged, on the morning that followed the steamboat disaster, in an elaborate toilet. He had mourned at length over some colored socks which his laundress had just returned in a bleached condition, owing to some vicious compound used in the washing, and was reflecting upon the disappointments of life, as he softened with powdered magnesia the over-rubicund tint which a liberal diet had begun to bestow upon his nose, when his valet burst into the room with a rumor of what had happened. Two or three general telegrams had been received, which, among other details, announced that Mr. Thorburn had been lost. Dana was terribly broken down by this information: even his interest in his personal appearance was pathetically subdued; and as soon as he could put himself decently together, he sallied forth to gain further particulars.

The report concerning Thorburn proved to be wrong; for both he and Perry were among the saved. There had been a great sacrifice of life, but, considering the nature of the calamity, a surprisingly large number of people had been rescued. When the New York papers arrived, after noon, with fuller accounts than had yet been received, the circumstance of one man attempting to force a mother and child away from their only means of safety was related, among various other startling and curious particulars which the survivors had given to correspondents, and roused general execrations; but Thorburn, being unknown to the mother — who had also reached the shore alive — was not identified as the wretch. He was in Newport by the time the papers came, and was met by a great many telegrams and sundry effusive callers, congratulating him on his personal good fortune.

Perry remained at Watch Hill, the nearest inhabited point on the coast, whither the rescued had been conveyed, and where many bodies of the drowned either floated in or were brought ashore. He was looking for some trace of Oliphant. . . .

Late in the afternoon he entered Newport, completely exhausted, and drove in a hired carriage slowly up Pelham Street, unwilling to go to his father's house, and bent upon engaging some bachelor quarters which he knew had been vacated a few days before. It was a lovely afternoon: the declining sun sent long, reddish rays between the old white houses, soft beams that caught the light dust and gave it a tint as delicate as peach-bloom or smote the outstretched branches of trees, and woke them to strange ardor of coloring, set off by the cool green in shadow and the first dull brown of changing foliage. A scanty drift of fallen leaves was blown occasionally along the sidewalks by the September wind, with a dry, rattling whisper. The sunbeams twinkled, too, upon the turning wheel-spokes that were plying on the avenue, as Perry reached the Park. A pink-coated fox-hunter crossed the head of the street, with his nag at a walk, holding his hunting-crop languidly, and exhibiting himself in a light of meritorious and manly fatigue: he was doing the heroic, for the benefit of that sybaritic society which rolled by him so suavely in the comfort of its stylish turnouts. Newport was still itself: smiling, serene, light-hearted; rejoicing in the gentle gratification of being almost English. But the sight did not soothe Perry: it sickened him. Life at Newport, which a few days before had seemed so proud, so splendid and fair, became suddenly in his eyes a pretentious patchwork, a thing of gorgeous shreds and tatters, gay as a fool's motley, and covering only a mass of petty or flippant traits of character, bound together by a restless desire for superficial pleasure. He had just been brought face to face with the most fearful realities; he had witnessed an act of perfect self-sacrifice; and now, as he came from that experience, with a burden of unspeakable sorrow on his heart, this world of ostentatious levity was a positive offence to him.

He obtained the rooms he wanted, sent for his own servant, and some clothes from his father's house, and then despatched messengers to ascertain where he could see Josephine; lying down, meanwhile, to rest.

During the two days since she had written to Oliphant, Octavia's mood had been brightening. The

fine warm ivory of her cheeks took on a delicate tinge
of rose; her vivacity, always fresh and in force, was
exquisitely, unconsciously, varied by a tremor of feeling, a more genial ardor of sympathy with every one
and with every thing that was going on, which made
it doubly enchanting. She did not dare to hope much;
she scarcely reflected at all; the claims of the past
upon her and the question of loyalty to Gifford's
memory retained no hold. She confessed nothing except that she was possessed by a sweet prescience that
soon she should be at peace with Oliphant and united
to him. On the night when he set out upon his journey
to Newport, she went to a large ball given by the
Spanish minister — one of the last and most iridescent
phases of the expiring season. The entertainment
was dazzling in the highest degree. An immense tent
had been connected with the minister's house, extending over a large stretch of lawn; and in the interior,
walled with an odorous wilderness of extravagant plants
in flower, the dancing took place, on a floor of perfect
smoothness, made for the occasion. The weather was
warm, and both in order to cool the place and for the
sake of decoration, a grotto of ice had been contrived
at the farther end, through which changing lights of
blue and green and yellow fire were thrown at intervals, transforming the glittering blocks to a fluorescent
mass. The whole house was spectacular in the richness and glow of its appointments, its illuminations,
its floral adornment; and the dense assembly that circulated through it flashed and shone with a fabulous
magnificence of beautiful costumes and sparkling jew-

els. Octavia took her place in the scene as a natural part of it, and held her own with ease. She drew quietly to herself the best of attention; she danced frequently, with the greatest enjoyment; and those who had seen most of her noticed the uncommon buoyancy of her talk and bearing.

Yet, when the hour came for going away, she herself was surprised at the subtile depression that weighed upon her. The ice-grotto had begun to melt, and was on the point of collapse; the chemical lights had faded; and at just about that time, the last satiated flames that had consumed the steamer on the Sound were throwing their exhausted ribbons of fire into the melancholy air.

In her room, Octavia remained awake for a while, to hear the approach of the boat; but its ominous though welcome roll of thunder from the booming paddles did not come to her ears. The failure made her somewhat uneasy, yet at last she fell asleep, without being able to explain it, and slept on until near noon. When she woke, she had a conviction that Oliphant would appear before nightfall. She prepared herself for that meeting, with the half-shy yet tender and minute care that a woman uses — in a tribute almost devout to the lover's ideal of her — when she is on the eve of seeing the man she holds dearest. Not a detail of her personal appearance was decided upon, without reference to this great anticipation.

But alas, Oliphant did not come. On looking at her paper, which for a moment did not seem to her worth reading on a day that she believed was to be so joyously memorable, Octavia's fluttering expectations received an abrupt check; and soon, although she had heard not a syllable from Oliphant and no hint of him was given in the report of the disaster, her suspense became unbearable.

"Do you know," she asked Vivian, whom she immediately went to see, "whether Mr. Oliphant was on board?"

"Mr. Oliphant! What put that into your head?" the bride exclaimed. "Of course not. He's gone to California."

Octavia was bewildered, and began to be pained by an unforeseen anxiety lest he had not received her letter. She told Vivian of her writing; and then Vivian was puzzled, too. It was resolved between them that Craig should try, by telegraphing, to ascertain whether such a person as Eugene Oliphant had been among the passengers.

The answer came to him at length, in the night.

That same evening, also, Perry saw Josephine. She was visiting again in Newport; but as it was two or three hours before he slept off his fatigue, he did not arrive at the house until nine. When she met him, he was so pale, so haggard, so worn, that she started back in affright.

"What is it?" she cried. "I heard of the accident, after your messenger came. Was your father really lost?"

"No," said Perry, his voice choking. "If you can come out, I will tell you."

Josephine threw a light wrap over her shoulders, and

they emerged into the grounds, which were near those of Octavia's villa. Without a word he walked down towards the water, and she followed him. They could see the bay dancing softly, mystically, in the light of the new moon, while the boundary-trees in front of them blotted the silvery radiance with a pattern of black, twisted trunks, sharply and uncouthly distinct. Then Perry paused.

"It was not my father," he said. "It was Oliphant who was lost."

A cry of horror and of suffering escaped from Josephine's lips; she leaned forward, and hid her face upon her arm, against one of the trees. For the first instant, her emotion seemed to Perry only what he might have expected; but it lasted so long that he began to question. With a rush, then, the truth came to his mind.

"You loved that man!" he exclaimed.

She lifted her head, at this, and met his intense, jealous scrutiny without wavering. There was a riddle in her eyes, still, as there always had been, and doubtless always would be; and in this semi-obscurity of the night it was more than ever hopeless to attempt solving that riddle. Her face was very white, he could see; yet he could almost have doubted whether the voice which answered him came from the softly moving lips, or from the shadows that surrounded her.

"Yes," it whispered. "I loved him."

Something like an imprecation rose to Perry's lips, but he only groaned: "I wish I could have died in his place!"

"You mustn't say that," Josephine returned, with strange calmness, though speaking hardly above her breath. "You have no right to wish it."

"Why?" he demanded, bitterly.

"Because it was fate. You must accept what fate brings."

"Ah, if it had brought me *you!*" he began, in a passionate way. "But no! You never could have married me; and even if things were different, I could hardly offer myself to you now." He went on rapidly, pouring out an account of the catastrophe and his father's brutal conduct. "After that," he said, "how should I hope to win a woman like you? The son of such a father! I suppose I have the same traits in me, somewhere."

"But you're not like him," Josephine returned, coming suddenly to his defence, against himself. "If you were you wouldn't condemn him."

"Then you think there's some chance for me?" he asked, giving way to a slight laugh of scorn. It was succeeded by a burst of earnest entreaty. "Oh, Josephine," he cried, "is there any hope, any possibility, that I may win you by and by? I will be content with any love you can give, if you think you might be happier with me than without me. Only let me know if I may keep this hope before my mind!"

"I cannot speak of it now," she said, in her mysterious tone, that was neither cold nor warm, but neutral, and shuddering a little. "It may be *our* fate—but not now; not now." After a silence she asked, "Is this what you came here to say?"

"No," he assured her. "I want you to help me in a difficult task. This news must be broken to Octavia."

He then explained to her, that he had found upon Oliphant, tightly folded in a letter case within a covered pocket, the note Octavia had sent him. It was somewhat water-soaked, but legible still, and Perry had guessed, from the few lines that caught his eye, something of the events which had inspired it.

Josephine consented to go with him to High Lawn, and he waited outside the door, while she went in to see Octavia.

"It is all over, Octavia," she said, quietly, as the widow entered to greet her. "You and I have been separated lately; but there is no need of it any more."

Octavia came up and caught her arm, with a quick apprehensive demand for her meaning. Briefly and tenderly, as well as she could, Josephine imparted every thing.

Octavia took the blurred letter, and glanced at it for an instant; then sank into a chair, gazing wanly at the woman who stood motionless opposite her. She shrank, and seemed to wither visibly.

"O God, O God!" she cried. "I have killed him. And how I am punished! That it should be my letter brought back to me, and that you, Josephine, should be the one to bring it!"

A heart-broken moan buried any thing further that she might have been moved to say, and the tears streamed from beneath her eyelids.

Oliphant was interred at Woodlawn, beside little Effie; and Octavia, without vehemence, but resolutely, and setting aside every conventional consideration, took her share in all the final dispositions. With Justin she went to place the flowers around him in his coffin, and looked once more upon her hapless lover. His face was not like that of a dead man; it was that of one who had been awakened and told that he might depart from imprisonment. True, the sinister and perhaps ironical change which comes over the countenances of those who are to open their lips no more on earth had fallen upon it. But through the baffling dumbness of its slightly pinched lines — that peculiar silence that seemed to be voluntary, like a mask put on in order that the wearer might conceal some intelligence too important to be betrayed by a look — there stole a far-off, wonderful, calm light of exalted joy.

What had he last thought of, as he passed away? She imagined the noble scorn that must have swept through every vein and nerve, when he measured the monstrous selfishness of old Thorburn, and instantly threw into the balance against it his own sacrifice. The final consciousness in his mind must have been one of absolute, magnanimous love; not for her, nor for any one individual, but a sentiment so large and ideal that it made the laying down of his life for a woman he had never seen before, and for her little child, a pleasure surpassing any other. Whether that woman was valuable in herself or not, she came before him in that tragic hour as a type of motherhood, she presented to him an image of life in its most sacred form; and the love in his heart went out towards it with perfect purity and power.

Such were the broken meditations that came to Octavia, while she arranged the flowers. She performed the task without flinching; yet a few irrepressible tears fell softly upon her hands, and the hands trembled slightly, like leaves wet with dew, just stirring in the breath of daybreak.

A year later, Octavia was again at Newport for a few days, soon after the season began. The place was still beautiful to her, and she remembered her old enthusiasm for it; but the spectacle of its life no longer held any charm. And yet how short a time since she had been a part of it! Was it out of that vanity and frivolity that her own folly had arisen, which led her to jest maliciously with Oliphant's love?

Once while she was there, she saw Josephine and Perry Thorburn driving together, and was conscious in a dreamy way of the fact, which had been imparted to her, that they were engaged; but she had no meeting with them.

Much more important and distinct to her mind was a long, kind letter which she received from Vivian Craig, written in Germany, whither Justin had gone after Oliphant's legacy was made over to him.

"I am wearing your diamonds that you gave me for a wedding present," said Vivian in her letter, "and baby has been crying for them. Just as I write, though, she is laughing again at their pretty sparkle."

So, in the quick round of life, the widow's tears had

become the moment's plaything of a child, and a rainbow coloring flashed from them.

The last day that Octavia spent in Newport, she went out on foot, and walked over the bleak downs where Oliphant had wandered on that dreary day of his defeat. She arrived at the great house near the cave; but the place was closed and empty now, and she could go down to the rocks without intrusion. For a long while she sat lost in thought upon the lonely little ledge on which, when she last visited it, Oliphant had sat with her. It was very silent there; the waters hardly murmured in the cave: no one was near. What an immense solitude surrounded her! And how much greater was the solitude of her own heart! Yet she felt a presence attending her: the soft breeze, that crept up to her and tenderly played with a tress or two of straying hair upon her forehead, was like Oliphant's hand caressing her. The slumbering ocean, too, which had absorbed his life, seemed conscious of him.

But had he not once loved another woman, and she another man? Which was the true love? She could not unravel the knot; but at least she knew that, whatever the limitations of one heart or of individual devotion, the great ideal passion survived through all these changes. Oliphant had brought something of rare worth into her life; had given her a higher conception of love. To this extent she shared in it, that it had touched her in passing, and that she now knew its quality. Though she had failed to grasp and keep it, the power and the fragrance remained with her still, like the lingering, lifting odor of the sea blown in at random through an artificial atmosphere.

Love had come, and love had gone. How strange that it had not staid with Oliphant, who so well deserved to have it! How strange that he should have chosen to follow her, instead of Josephine; and that Josephine's passion for him should have been so blindly frustrated! Octavia herself was also left alone. And yet, though love had thus come and gone, it was somehow here at last.

Octavia rose from the ledge to walk back: she was about to leave Newport forever. As she stood for a moment there, her small, fine figure was relieved against the gray bastion of rock like a silhouette.

She was clad wholly in black — black never more to be abandoned.

A New Story by the Author of "Guerndale."

THE CRIME OF HENRY VANE.

By "J. S. of Dale."

1 Volume. 12mo, - - $1.

"Henry Vane" is a study of American life. It is worth while to note, in the midst of the present flood of literature dealing with the inexhaustible problem of the American girl, that here is a different phase of the American girl from any that is familiar—a more serious one, if not one that every reader will be willing to accept as true. The story is told with the vivid and strong simplicity that has been a distinguishing trait of the author's power; and while the plot contains a great surprise, none of the force of the narrative is sacrificed merely to this.

*** *For sale by all booksellers, or sent, postpaid, on receipt of price by*

CHARLES SCRIBNER'S SONS,

743 and 745 Broadway, New York.

www.ingramcontent.com/pod-product-compliance
Lightning Source LLC
Chambersburg PA
CBHW032043230426
43672CB00009B/1449